INTRODUCTION

TO THE

TEACHING OF LIVING LANGUAGES

WITHOUT

GRAMMAR OR DICTIONARY.

BY

L. SAUVEUR, Ph.D., LL.D.

BOSTON:

SCHŒNHOF & MŒLLER; LEE & SHEPARD;
A. WILLIAMS & CO.

NEW YORK: F. W. CHRISTERN.

1875.

Cambridge:
Press of John Wilson & Son.

PREFACE.

This pamphlet is designed to accompany the book entitled, "Causeries avec mes élèves." Here is the preface of the work.

"The book that I am to-day publishing has been often solicited of me by my pupils. It is dedicated to them as a *souvenir* of our pleasant intercourse. They were before my eyes while I was writing, and I have heard them answering and questioning me. Nor is it exactly a book: in that is its character and its value. It is nothing but a simple conversation vividly put upon paper, and which has almost retained its gestures. My pupils will see me in reading it, as I have seen them in composing it. I converse there only with this little company, charming and select, curious to know every thing in the world of ideas, of things, and of literature. The persons who will employ it for the study of French, will learn there a rich and varied language; at the same time they will cultivate their minds and elevate their thoughts.

" If I am not under a delusion, my work answers a real need, and will one day become the manual of all the schools. Foreigners who are studying French wish to speak. This book, and no other, leads to this result. The professors of Harvard, and those of Yale, have appreciated the system which it reproduces, and have acknowledged it superior to every other. This was already the judgment of Montaigne three centuries ago.

" The book is new and original: like my lessons, it teaches the language without grammar or dictionary; like them also, it speaks French from the first hour, and does not pronounce one word of English.

" It is intended for my pupils and for all those who teach and study my language; it is addressed none the less to persons eager for knowledge; they will find there a whole world of things and ideas. The analytical table with which it closes, presents a striking *tableau* of it.

" In spite of appearances, there is in the book a perfect order and a never-broken chain. I also beg my readers to commence at the first page; I am confident that they will stop only at the end.

" As the book is new, I accompany it with a pamphlet translated into English under my supervision It explains how it is to be employed in classes.

" If this double work contribute to elevate the teaching of the languages, to free it from its deplorable routine, I shall be sufficiently rewarded for my efforts, and happy in having accomplished a useful work." [1]

This preface is sufficient, nor was even this perhaps necessary, to teach how the book is to be used, as far as regards the nine or ten American ladies who have attended my classes, and who are teaching French as I do myself. But for the sake of those persons unacquainted with the system of the School of Modern Languages of Boston, it seems useful to give a few explanations. Another reason which leads me to write this pamphlet is, that it furnishes me with the means of addressing myself to the public in English. In my book, English could have no place, since it has none in my lessons. And yet I wished to speak to the Committees of schools, as also to the persons who are ignorant of the language and who desire to study it. I hope above all, by this pamphlet, to

[1] Professor Heness's book, " The Teaching of German without Grammar or Dictionary," will be published before Oct. 1.

aid my brother teachers in applying with success a method which will insure to them as much pleasure as the old routine has inspired them with distaste.

It would be easy for me to write a large book on the methods, and to make it a work of erudition. I refrain from it, to consider only my readers' interests. My pages will be both simple and practical.

INTRODUCTION TO TEACHING WITHOUT GRAMMAR OR DICTIONARY.

I.

THE FIRST LESSON.

THE most beautiful lesson that I can imagine of any kind, and assuredly the most interesting that there can be, is the first lesson given to a class learning a language without grammar. There is no orator, were it even Demosthenes, who can hold a public more attentive, more eagerly expectant of every word, than the professor who is giving this first lesson. Not one of his movements is lost. His word, his eye, his gesture, his whole person speaks; and he is in possession of the undivided mind of those who are before him. During two or three hours, neither they nor he have had a single distraction, even for a second. I have never seen, either at the foot of the pulpit of Père Lacordaire or of the tribune of M. Thiers, listeners as attentive and absorbed as mine have been every time that I have commenced a course.

Is it astonishing, think you? and is there a work more interesting than this, or a greater? Learned professors have sometimes done me the honor to say, "How is it possible that a man of letters can find pleasure in teaching even the elements?" In truth, they did not understand my pleasure, because they had not seen this lesson, and did not surmise that it is the most exalted of all. I have never found in any of my lessons of literature or of æsthetics, nor in any of my lectures, even the most enthusiastic, half of the satisfaction that a first lesson gives me. It puts me under a spell, and holds my listeners there.

What is then, this lesson? It is a conversation during two hours *in the French language* with twenty persons who know nothing of this language. After five minutes only, I am carrying on a dialogue with them, and this dialogue does not cease. It continues the following days, and ends only the last day of the year. Not a word of English is pronounced, and every thing is understood, and all talk. I have never seen a single pupil who did not understand and talk from this first hour.

Does one understand now the interest of this lesson, and is one still astonished that the teacher does not find the pleasure of giving it beneath him? Have I not, besides, to hold conversation with an intelligent audience, which at the end of fifteen or twenty days, has sufficiently given me its ear so that I can speak of the most elevated subjects. Open my book at the ninth or tenth lesson, and say if you find the subjects unworthy of yourself, however learned and enlightened you may be. An eminent minister of this city visiting, one day, one of my classes at the tenth lesson, being asked what subject he wished to hear me discuss with my class, chose *God*. I talked for an hour with my pupils, without a single answer being refused me. "It is admirable," said he; "I see the thing: it is done; how, I cannot imagine." It is natural; he had not seen us advance from the first day from the known to the unknown, never letting drop our chain of words, and increasing every minute our little vocabulary.

But your vocabulary is nothing the first day, one objects. How can one go from the known to the unknown, when the known is zero? Without doubt, the known in French is zero, and I cannot start from nothing. But do you not know that there is a language which is yours and mine, without being English or French, — the language of all, the admirable language of gesture? Very well! I raise quickly my finger before you, and show it to you. Do you not understand, whatever your language may be, that that means *there is the finger?* And if I point my extended forefinger towards the table or the door, do you not understand that I say, *There is the table ; there is the door?* And if, on showing you the finger, I say in my French language, *Voilà le doigt*, do you not understand that the French pronounce these words to indicate that thing? There is my dictionary commenced, and now you understand me instantly, if I continue by saying to you, *There is the forefinger ; there is the book*, etc. Then I count my ten fingers, and you count with me, always in French. We find ten fingers on our hands, and immediately I show them to you; and, drawing an inference from our numeration, I turn my forefinger towards myself, pronouncing these words, *I have ten fingers ;* and I add instantly, pointing my finger towards you, *You have ten fingers, madame.* Immediately I commence to make you speak, by asking you how many fingers you have, and you answer, *I have ten fingers.* To a second question, *How many fingers have I?* you answer me, *You have ten fingers.* From this time, the dialogue advances without ceasing again.

I reproduce for those who are ignorant of French, the

first and the second lessons of the book. Place before you a teacher who speaks with word and with gesture, and you will understand as my pupils understand.

There are in the first lesson one hundred and twenty or one hundred and thirty words, and all this vocabulary is in the full possession of the class the first day, with the sounds which they produce, and the gesture which accompanies them. It is a serious acquisition. After this first day, the professor has only to go forward. without ever pronouncing a single word of English, never ceasing to pass from the known to the unknown, never omitting a link in the chain, and never losing sight of his object. If he follow my book, and take note of this advice, he will succeed as well as I; he will be, like me, enthusiastic over his teaching, and will find in it delights which he did not anticipate. His lungs will be fatigued perhaps, sometimes; but at least his mind will never be, and his soul will experience no weariness. One hour of repose will restore his chest, while nothing can solace him for the *ennui* which grammars cause him: this is a suffering which kills, or at least shortens life, and takes from the mind all freshness and vigor.

THE FINGERS.

"Here is the finger. Look. Here is the forefinger, here is the middle finger, here is the ring-finger, here is the little finger, and here is the thumb. Do you see the finger, madame? Yes, you see the finger, and I see the finger. Do you see the finger, monsieur? — Yes, I see the finger. — Do you see the forefinger, madame? — Yes, I see the forefinger. — And you, monsieur? You see the forefinger, and I also. And you, my little boy? — And I also. — And you, mademoiselle? — And I also. — You all see the forefinger, and the thumb, and the middle finger. Do you see the little finger also, monsieur? — Yes. — Let us count the fingers : one, two, three, four, five, six, seven, eight, nine, ten. We have ten fingers. I have ten fingers ; you have ten fingers, mademoiselle. How many fingers have you, madame? — I have ten fingers. — And you, monsieur? — And I also. — And George? — And George also. — Do you see the ten fingers? — Yes. — Let us count the fingers together... That is right.

" The thumb is the first finger, the forefinger is the second, the middle finger is the third, the ring-finger is the fourth, and the little finger is the fifth. Which is the third finger? Which is the fifth?

" The thumb is near the forefinger, the little finger is near the ring-finger. Where is the thumb, madame? — The thumb is near the forefinger. — And the middle finger? — The middle finger is near the forefinger and near the ring-finger. — That is very well.

There is a table and a chair. Do you see the table? — Yes. — How many tables do you see? — One. — Where is the chair? — The chair is near the table. — And the table? — Near the chair. — And where am I? — Near the table and near the chair. — The forefinger is between the thumb and the middle finger ; the ring-finger is between the middle finger and the little finger.

There is an arm-chair. Where is the arm-chair? — The arm-chair is near the chair. — And the chair? — The chair is between the table and the arm-chair. — That is right, you understand. In French, arm-chair (*fauteuil*) is masculine ; chair (*chaise*) is feminine, and table (*table*) also. It is strange, is it not? We have ten fingers in

France; you also in America. But you have three genders, the masculine, the feminine, and the neuter. We have
the masculine and feminine; not the neuter.

" All the fingers except the thumb have three phalanges;
the thumb has only two phalanges. Here they are. Between two phalanges, there is a joint.

" The nail is at the end of the finger. How many nails
have we, madame? Answer. It is easy: we have ten
fingers; consequently we have ten nails.

" Let us continue. The thumb is thick, strong, and short.
The middle finger is thick, strong, and long. The ring-
finger is not strong; it is weak. Weak is the opposite of
strong, and long the opposite of short. Do you understand,
mesdames? — Yes, monsieur. — Is the thumb long? — No.
— Is it strong or weak? — It is strong. — And the ring-
finger? — It is weak. — Is monsieur strong or weak? — He
is strong. — And you, too, my little friend? — Yes.

" The forefinger is shorter than the middle finger; the
middle finger is longer than the forefinger, and longer than
the ring-finger. The middle finger is the longest of all
the fingers, the thumb is the strongest, and the ring-finger is the weakest. It is a poor finger, is it not? — Yes. —
Is the little finger stronger than the thumb? — No. — On
the contrary, mesdames, it is less strong. Less is the opposite of more. Is the thumb more or less long than the
forefinger? — It is less long. — My young friend, is mademoiselle more or less strong than monsieur? — She is less
strong. — And you? — And I also. — And I? — I do
not know. — *Forte* (strong) is the feminine of *fort*. Be
attentive to my pronunciation. Monsieur is very strong.
He is strong in the highest degree. Madame is less strong
than monsieur. Less expresses inferiority, more marks

superiority. Are you fatigued, mesdames? — Yes, very much fatigued. — That is right, you use the superlative, and you understand. Let us rest five minutes. — Ten, sir. — I am very willing.

"I can bend, stretch out, move the fingers. See: I bend the forefinger; I stretch out the forefinger; I move the five fingers. Bend your fingers, my young friend. What are you doing? — I am bending my fingers. — Stretch them out; move them. That is right. Can you bend the chair? — No. — Can you move the table? — Yes. — Can you count the fingers? — Yes, I can count them. — Count them. Let us count them together. Imitate my pronunciation. Let us count again. That is right. The lesson is finished. Adieu, mesdames.

THE HANDS.

" It is nine o'clock precisely; let us commence.

"The fingers belong to the hand. Here is one hand; here are two hands. Do you see the two hands? — Yes, I see them. — I have two hands, a right hand and a left hand; you have two hands; madame has two hands; we all have two hands, thanks to God. Where is the right hand? — Here it is. — And the left hand? — Here it is. — How many hands have you, my friend? — I have two hands. — And I? — You also. — Has the table also two hands? — No. — That is right, the table has no hands, nor the chair either. And the arm-chair? — Nor that either. — Stretch out the right hand....You do not understand? Can you stretch out the fingers? — Yes, monsieur. — Very well! you can stretch out the hands also. Can you not? — Yes. — Stretch out the right hand then. That is it.

of its powerlessness in Europe as in America, of the defects in its methods. In your country, you tell me, Messrs. Jules Simon and Michel Bréal have just published writings in which they point out the poverty of teaching. Yes, and their books themselves distress us by their timidity and their inefficiency. I have not found there any hope of a radical change, and it is such a revolution that is needed at any price. But it is not for me to speak, at this time at least, of the reform of our colleges and our universities. When the teaching of the modern languages shall have entered upon the right path, that of the ancient languages will necessarily follow sooner or later.

Have you invented your system, I am asked also. Certainly not; I have not that glory: it is very old, for it dates back perhaps to Socrates, and, very surely, at least to Rabelais and Montaigne. As for me, I had seen it at these great sources when I came to this country. I had made some incomplete trials of it in the teaching of Greek and Latin. I had a horror of the sterile instruction by the grammar. I had, like everybody else, been its victim at college and in the university. I remember, vividly, having in my class of rhetoric, after six years of suffering and disgust, thrown into the fire, with delight, my Latin grammar, the day on which I understood the subjunctive, by dint of reading Cæsar, which I had persisted in studying constantly, not giving it up even for Cicero and the poets.

Arriving in this country, I had the good fortune to meet at New Haven Professor Heness, to-day my colleague in the School of Modern Languages. He was practising there, with a marvellous success, the system of Montaigne. He had found the light that I was seeking, and communicated to me the means of teaching the Americans my language, without submitting them to the tortures of which I had been the victim. I would express to him here my profound gratitude. A single hour's conversation with him revealed to me all the practicability of this admirable system, of which I knew only the theory; and I decided with enthusiasm to employ it.

The experience I have had for five years has been so flattering that I will not speak of it, even while declaring that I attribute no portion of my success to my personal merit, and that all the honor belongs to the system. This — is my conviction; and it is for this motive that I am striving to make it understood and adopted by all those who are wishing to teach or to acquire a foreign language.

I might say much here of Socrates and of Montaigne, might say that the Greek philosopher passed with his disciples from the known to the unknown, discussing incessantly with them; that the admirable dialogues of Plato are a charming image of this sublime teaching; that it is these dialogues which have best taught me the art of questioning a pupil and of making him speak: but this subject would be too long to develop here.

As for Montaigne, I will say a little more. I cannot do better, in order not to permit myself to be drawn into a theoretical discussion, than to reproduce simply one of the chapters of my book, entitled, "The Face. — Montaigne." My readers will see there, at the same time, one of my lessons in its original form.

THE FACE. — MONTAIGNE.

"There is a mirror on the wall, between the two windows. Do you see it, monsieur? — No. — I believe you indeed; it is behind you. Rise and turn round. That is right. The mirror is before you now. Do you see it? — Yes, I see it. — Where is it? — It is between the windows hanging on the wall. — I see myself in it; do you see yourself in it? — I see myself in it also. *Je m'y vois; vous y voyez-vous?* — *Je m'y vois aussi.* I imitate you, monsieur; but you do not explain what *y* signifies. — Certainly not; I do not wish to explain. One does not understand explanations when one commences the study of a language. — What am I to do, monsieur? — Listen, I beg you: imitate me, as you said, and understand by guessing a little. — What does *y* signify in this case? — Tell monsieur, mademoiselle. — It signifies, I think, I see myself in the mirror. But why do you speak of the mirror, when you announce the face? — It is to speak French and to teach it to you. I needed to put the word mirror in my chain. — Pardon me, monsieur, I know that you are always right, and that we understand you without dictionary or grammar. I make objections in order to talk. — The very thing! Talk, talk a great deal. Remember our motto, *Fit fabricando faber.* Do you know Montaigne? — No, monsieur. — And Shakespeare. — Oh, yes indeed! — Had he a library? — How can one doubt it, he who knew every thing! — That is right, but he did not learn every thing from books. Did he read Montaigne? — I do not know. — He did read him; his copy of Montaigne's Essays is in the British Museum with his signature. — Do we know the other books of the great poet? — No, mademoiselle; we know only this one book of Shakspeare. — Are you sure of it monsieur? — I trust to Mr. Emerson. It is a good authority, is it not? — Excellent.

" Read his beautiful study entitled, ' Montaigne or the Skeptic.' — In which volume, monsieur ? — In ' Representative Men.' Are you not acquainted with it ? — No, I have heard it spoken of. — Then you are not acquainted with all of Emerson ? — Certainly not. — And you have read the whole of Dickens's works ? — Yes. — Alas! you do not put your hand on the great books, on those which enlighten, which elevate, which inspire, which lead one to think. You will never read Emerson enough. Will you listen to some good advice ? — Yes, very willingly. — Read immediately that beautiful, that grand chapter, ' Books,' in the volume ' Society and Solitude.'

" But I was speaking of Montaigne. — When did he live? — In the sixteenth century. — Three centuries ago. — Yes, and three centuries ago he studied a foreign language, an ancient language even, without dictionary or grammar, as you are studying French. — Is it possible? — Yes, madame; have we advanced much since Montaigne in teaching? — I do not know. — What! do you not see our position? — No. — Montaigne is in advance; we are in the background. — How did he learn Latin? — Listen, he began when he was quite young. — Who was his teacher? — A German. — Did he speak French well? — Fortunately not; he did not know a word of it. — What did he do? — He spoke Latin. — Did he explain the lessons to the little boy? — Impossible, since he did not have French at his command. — Had he a grammar? — Neither grammar nor dictionary, Montaigne tells us in chapter xxv. of the ' Essays.' — What did the little boy do? — He did just as you are doing. He listened to his teacher; he answered his teacher; and like you he was curious and asked questions. — Did he speak French with

his father and mother? — Not a word.   French was prohibited in the castle of Montaigne, as English is prohibited
here. — Did the family speak Latin? — Yes, as well as
they could.   All were forbidden to speak French in
presence of the little boy.   Father, mother, servants,
waiting-maids were to speak Latin or use gestures. —
Did this instruction succeed? — Listen to Montaigne himself: 'I learned Latin without a book, without a grammar
or rules, and I spoke it as well as my teacher.' — It is
wonderful, monsieur. — Pardon! It is natural.   You have
children, madame? — Yes, I have two. — How old are
they? — They are five and a half years old. — You mean,
one is five and a half.   And the other? — Is five and a
half too. — Ah! I understand.   They are twins, *jumeaux*.
— Yes, monsieur, two good little girls. — They are *ju-
melles* (feminine) in that case.   Do they speak English? —
As well as I do. — And better than I? — Yes. — Yet I
know the grammar better than they. — No matter, they
speak much better than you do. — Is it wonderful? — No,
it is natural. — It was the same for Montaigne, and here
we are of the same mind, I hope.   It is sufficient to explain ourselves to agree.

"But, let us see! how did we commence our lesson? —
With the mirror, monsieur. — That is it, my friend.   And
how did we leave the mirror? — It was the fault of
mademoiselle. — It was no fault.   What did she do then?
— She asked why you were speaking of the mirror. —
What did I answer? — I do not remember. — Assist the
little boy's memory, if you please, mesdames. — You said
that you wished to put the mirror in your chain. — That
is right; I have it.   I wished to say the face is the mirror
of the soul. — What is the soul? — It is the better half

of man. — The wife, monsieur ? — The wife ? — Why do you laugh, monsieur ? — Why ! it is capital, mademoiselle, you say a witty thing without knowing it. I will explain myself better next time."

We see that Montaigne has studied Latin as we are studying French, and with the same success. I do not desire at this time, I have already said, to occupy myself with the reform of the teaching of the ancient languages. Montaigne would lead the way to it admirably, and I have very often thought of it in presence of the deficiencies of our colleges. Unfortunately we are not radical in France, nor in Europe. Who would dare to speak there of a revolution in education? It is needed, however; an " Eighty-nine " is needed to destroy this world of errors which has lasted for centuries. I believe that it will be accomplished first in America, when it shall have been acknowledged necessary by a daring and intelligent man of this country, who will make himself the apostle of the reform. Truly, I am confident of this, the American being the most enterprising of men and the least given to routine. In France, one sees the learned professor of Latin, to whom the word revolution is pronounced, irritated on the spot. And in truth, does he not occupy his round on the ladder of instruction? What would become of him if this round were destroyed, or if his programme only were modified? Is he not a machine, learned it is true; and would he be able to do otherwise than he has done from the first day! Alas! This is no satire; I express, extenuating as I can, a sad truth. The professor in Europe, save in rare exceptions, is, in his chair, only an instrument, without initiative power, without originality, a man who has studied many books, but has not an idea of his own, and who would not be capable of doing any thing or of producing any thing, if you took from him his Latin grammar or his written explanations of Cicero.

Do you know what Montaigne says of him? He considers him the most contemptible of men, and is not astonished, on seeing his teaching, that the name of pedant is one of the most odious of the language. He is beneath the average of men; he is a blockhead, says he, who plunders science from books, and who has it only superficially on his lips. He does not do like the bee, who goes to gather sweets from the flowers, and makes therefrom a honey, a honey of its own. He knows well how to say, " Cicero, Aristotle or Plato said that." But what does he say and what does he decide for himself? Nothing. When I ask him what he knows, he calls for a book to show me. Pardon me these cruel revelations. It is Montaigne who speaks. Our pedant cannot say the simplest thing without going immediately to study his dictionary or his grammar. Nothing is made to penetrate his intelligence; he does like the man who has need of fire at home, who goes to the neighbor's, looks at the fire which is there, and never thinks of carrying any into his own house. There is the profit he makes of the grammar and dictionary. Here I quote the text of Montaigne: " That *savant*, as Plato said of the sophists, his brothers, is of all men the one who promises to be the most useful to men; whereas, among all men, he is the only one who not only does not improve what is confided to him, as does the carpenter or the mason, but makes it worse, and expects to be paid for having made it worse." When his pupil comes back from college, he is more senseless, he says, than when he left home seven years previously.

Before Montaigne, Rabelais had already given his opinion of our learned professor. Gargantua had studied long years under his tuition: his father perceived that the young giant was working really very well, that he was giving all his time to it; however he was profiting in no wise, and, what is worse, was becoming foolish and imbecile from it. The father saw then that the knowledge of the teacher was all nonsense, that his wisdom was only pretence, that he was debasing all noble minds, and corrupting all the flower of youth. He made an experiment, and placed his son in presence of a young boy of twelve years, who had not been subjected to the teaching of the *savant*. The boy reasoned wisely and eloquently on all subjects, while Gargantua " began to cry like a baby, and hid his face in his cap, and it was impossible to draw a word from him." The father was incensed, and would fain have killed the professor. They succeeded in calming him with great difficulty; he contented himself with discharging our pedant. But, as for us, we keep him still.

You have seen that Montaigne when a child was a true Latin, thanks to the method of teaching that we are practising; when a young man, he was sent to college, where, owing to the grammars and dictionaries, they made him half forget the language of Cæsar and Cicero.

But you yourself, have you a new idea, do you ask me, have you something to propose for the teaching of Latin? Yes, I have an idea, well matured, and that long ago; but of what use to give it; they will not put it in practice: it consists of a radical change, a revolution.   Here it is, however; I give it in closing, and without insisting upon it. This is not the place. The study of Latin takes in France, at college and in the university, from eight to ten years; I propose that two years be devoted to it, and to obtain a result even better. We enter the Latin school at ten years old; very well! at this time let the young man be placed in an institution, where he should pass two years. There should be known and spoken only the language of old Rome: neither French nor any other language should penetrate there. They should teach arithmetic, history, geography, etc., in Latin. For other books, only those of Latin writers should be read. They should do all day long, during two years, for Latin, what we are doing for French two or three hours a day during one year. Can you doubt of the result? At twelve years of age, the young student, without having suffered the torture of grammars, would know the language and even the grammar, as the sons of the Romans, and would be ready to continue in his own language all his studies with a well-informed, sound head and a mind strengthened by his intercourse with the strongest intelligences of antiquity. But I must close. I have said too much already, if all which precedes did not apply pertinently to our pupils in regard to French as it does to Montaigne with respect to Latin.

And what would you do with the Greek, am I asked? I have on this point also a very decided theory, but I will not enlarge upon it here, nor at this time. This question does not concern in any way the subject with which I am occupied.

III.

HOW THE BOOK IS TO BE USED.

HERE is a note from the book on this question.

"At the moment I was about to send these pages to the printer, a lady who teaches made me the following observation: 'I like very much your commencement,' said she, 'this will be a treasure for my pupils and for me. For you have converted me to your system. But are you not proceeding too rapidly? In this chapter on the *Hair*, will your pupil understand all that you say by means of what precedes?' This remark decided me to put the following note at the bottom of the page.

"It must be borne in mind that I always suppose the pupil to be led by an attentive and intelligent teacher. No book can quite take the place of oral instruction. Besides, my work is only a portion of the lesson to be given; it can guide the teacher, suggest to him ten questions where I give one, and also inspire the pupil, excite him to ask questions, and awaken his curiosity. This is the whole system of Socrates. If the teacher spend eight days on one of my lessons, he will have employed the time well. — They ask me also if the pupil is to read my book with his teacher. — My dear brother teachers, I have neither the right nor the pretension to prescribe to you any thing. Put your experience by the side of mine, and do whatever you deem most useful to your pupil. If, however, you wish to have my advice on this point, do as follows at the commencement; give your pupils the book to read at home, as a preparation for your teaching, but forbid them to open it in the class; their ear alone must be occupied there. When they are before you, put to them a hundred questions on the lesson of the book, and, if you wish, read to them yourself a page from the book, and make them understand every thing without ever pronouncing a word of English. There is the secret and the condition of success. This is a revolution in teaching, but it is necessary: it was three centuries ago that Rabelais and Montaigne asked for it. For three centuries every thing has advanced except teaching. Is it not humiliating for us?"

It is hardly necessary to say any thing further. Experience has taught me that all books should be withheld from the pupils for at least a month; that is to say, until the ear is accustomed to the sounds of the language. When they shall have talked with you for this length of time, without a word of English having been pronounced, you will be able with advantage to have them open the book in your classes. Until then, advise them to read the chapter that you are studying, at home, before and after your lessons. This reading will have excited their curiosity, and will bring them before you with questions which they will put to you; this will be the most interesting and the most useful part of your lesson. You will thus render active the mind of your pupils. This activity is an indispensable condition of their progress. The reading that you have prescribed for them will prevent them from being machines. With your grammars, they are nothing else. They gather sweets, but make no honey any more than their master. In reading the chapter again after the lesson, in their own room, they will fix in their mind the work you have been over together, will recall your discussions, and will bring you the next day new reflections and new questions.

After a month, when the class shall employ the book in your lessons, you will continue to examine every thing, to discuss every thing with the pupils, to bring out around you a thousand new thoughts; and you will find yourself, do not doubt it, as rich as you formerly were poor, and as interested and full of life as you were wearied and indifferent over your grammars and books, which have neither soul nor ideas. Neither you nor your pupils will be impatient for the end of the hour; it will take you by surprise and the time will be always too short.

If there are in my book affirmations with which you do not coincide, doubts where you would wish affirmations, opinions which are not yours, so much the better; you will refute them, you and your pupils will discuss them, and I shall have attained my end, — to put life into your classes, and numerous ideas into the heads of your pupils, together with that wealth of words which ideas carry with them.

I recommend also to my brother teachers to ask only earnest questions, which will render the class attentive and interested: nothing is more contemptible or more fruitless than phrases which are only phrases. They are even powerless to teach words. How can one have the courage to present to intelligent persons, to children even, in order to teach them the present of the indicative of the verb *avoir*, a *tableau* like the following? " *J'ai un chapeau; tu as un fromage; il a trois poires; mademoiselle a une rose; nous avons deux fourchettes, vous avez une robe; vos amis ont un chien, et vos sœurs ont un gros chat.*" I am almost ashamed of writing these stupid things, even to point them out to the ridicule of the public.

Another point that I recommend, is to connect scrupulously the questions in such a manner that one may give rise to another.

I reproduce here as examples, in the first place, a fable of La Fontaine which presents only questions and which I give in French; in the second place, I render in English the chapter entitled, "The Forehead. — Wendell Phillips."

LE COCHET, LE CHAT, ET LE SOURICEAU.

Un souriceau tout jeune, et qui n'avait rien vu,
    Fut presque pris au dépourvu.
Voici comme il conta l'aventure à sa mère.
J'avais franchi les monts qui bornent cet état,
    Et trottais comme un jeune rat
    Qui cherche à se donner carrière,
Lorsque deux animaux m'ont arrêté les yeux:
    L'un doux, bénin, et gracieux,
Et l'autre turbulent, et plein d'inquiétude;
    Il a la voix perçante et rude,
    Sur la tête un morceau de chair,
Une sorte de bras dont il s'élève en l'air
    Comme pour prendre sa volée,
    La queue en panache étalée.
Or, c'était un cochet, dont notre souriceau
    Fit à sa mère le tableau
Comme d'un animal venu de l'Amérique.
Il se battait, dit-il, les flancs avec ses bras,
    Faisant tel bruit et tel fracas,
Que moi, qui grâce aux dieux de courage me pique,
    En ai pris la fuite de peur,
    Le maudissant de très-bon cœur.
    Sans lui j'aurais fait connaissance
Avec cet animal qui m'a semblé si doux:
    Il est velouté comme nous,
Marqueté, longue queue, une humble contenance;

Un modeste regard, et pourtant l'œil luisant.
Je le crois fort sympathisant
Avec messieurs les rats ; car il a des oreilles
En figure aux nôtres pareilles.
Je l'allais aborder, quand d'un son plein d'éclat
L'autre m'a fait prendre la fuite.
Mon fils, dit la souris, ce doucet est un chat,
Qui, sous son minois hypocrite,
Contre toute ta parenté
D'un malin vouloir est porté.
L'autre animal, tout au contraire,
Bien éloigné de nous mal faire,
Servira quelque jour peut-être à nos repas.
Quant au chat, c'est sur nous qu'il fonde sa cuisine.

Garde-toi, tant que tu vivras,
De juger des gens sur la mine.

Qu'est-ce qu'un cochet ? — Et un souriceau ? — Quel est le·personnage principal de la fable ? — Nous représente-t-il ? — N'y-a-t-il pas une souris en scène ? — Quel est le plus sage des deux, le souriceau ou la souris ? — Pourquoi ? — Le souriceau avait-il vu le monde ? — Avait-il de l'expérience ? — Pensez-vous qu'il juge bien le monde la première fois qu'il le verra ? — Ne sommes-nous pas comme lui ? — Est-il dangereux pour lui de mal juger ? — Et pour nous ?

L'état, le pays du souriceau et de sa mère, est-il grand ? — Et notre pays, et notre monde ? — Le monde de la souris n'est-il pas grand à ses yeux ? — Le monde de la souris et notre monde sont-ils beaucoup plus grands l'un que l'autre aux yeux de Dieu ? — Nos monts et nos océans ne sont-ils pas pour lui comme les monts qui bornent l'état des souris ?

Que signifie *se donner carrière* ? — Les chevaux des Grecs ne couraient-ils pas dans la carrière d'Olympie ?

Quelle est la première expérience du souriceau dans le monde ? — Qui rencontre-t-il ? — Quelle description fait-il du chat ? — Et du jeune coq ? — Lequel préfère-t-il ? — Pourquoi aime-t-il le chat ? — Pourquoi a-t-il peur du coq ? — A-t-il jugé sur la mine ? — A-t-il bien jugé ? — A-t-il vu un hypocrite ? — L'a-t-il reconnu pour un hypocrite ? — Ne jugeons-nous pas comme lui, quand nous entrons dans la vie ? — Rencontrons-nous des hypocrites ? — Les reconnaissons-nous ? — Sont-ils dangereux ? — En sommes-nous dupes quelquefois ? — Le chat pour les souris et Tartufe pour nous, est-ce la même chose ? — Molière aimait-il Tartufe ? — La vieille souris n'a-t-elle pas signalé le chat, l'hypocrite à son enfant ? — Et La Fontaine nous signale-t-il les Tartufes ? — Le souriceau profitera-t-il de la leçon de sa mère ? — Profiterez-vous de celle de La Fontaine, mon ami ? — Un bon drôle comme le coq est-il à craindre ? — Et les hommes qui sont comme lui ? — Aimez-vous les chats, petite fille ? — Aimez-vous les hommes-chats, madame ? — Il n'y a pas de femmes-chats, n'est-ce pas, mesdames ?

Quelle est la morale de notre fable ? — La mine n'est-elle pas l'image de l'âme ? — Ne devrait-elle pas l'être ?

Ecoutez une petite histoire à ce sujet.

Victor Considérant, un socialiste fameux qui croyait au progrès de l'espèce humaine, à ses transformations, avait été frappé de ce fait que la ·mine peut tromper. " Par la mine nous ne lisons pas dans les âmes, disait-il, et nous ne voyons pas la grimace qu'on fait à notre dos après

nous avoir fait une révérence et un compliment par devant. Il y a là un double vice de notre nature. Quand
nous serons plus parfaits, nous verrons dans les cœurs et
nous aurons un œil derrière." C'était ingénieux, trop
ingénieux. Le lendemain de cette découverte de Considérant, Le Charivari de Paris se moqua et nous fit rire.
Il avait représenté un bel homme avec une queue superbe
terminée par une riche touffe de cheveux, et au milieu de
cette touffe un œil de bœuf. C'était l'homme de l'avenir,
l'homme de V. Considérant.

Croyez-vous à cet homme-là, mademoiselle ? — Pouvons-
nous espérer avoir une queue un jour ? — Ne devrons-
nous pas nous contenter toujours de l'œil de l'expérience ?

THE FOREHEAD. — WENDELL PHILLIPS.

It is this part of the face. — Which ? — Oh ! mademoiselle, you look at your bouquet, charming distraction, but
a distraction after all. I claim your ears for my words and
your eyes for my gestures. — Pardon me, monsieur. — I
have put my finger on my forehead. See ! If I were
ever writing our lessons for those who are not here, would
they understand them ? — I think not. — Why ? — Because
you speak by gesture constantly. — Well ? — You cannot
write your gesture. — But if my reader imagine my gesture ? — How imagine it ? — That's true. But what is to
be done ? — Print a forehead in your book. — What nonsense you are talking ! But if my reader have an intelligent professor, who will guide him and show him as I
do ? — Oh ! then he will understand every thing. The
French gesticulate much, do they not, monsieur ? — Yes,

much. They have the eloquence of gesture. Their gesture speaks. Do you wish an anecdote on this subject? — Yes; I like your anecdotes. They always explain something. — Very well! here is one.

One day the duc de la Rochefoucauld, in his extreme old age, was having a *tête à tête* with a lady as old as he. The lady said, " Monsieur le duc, it seems that Death has forgotten you and me." O the gods! If Death were listening, if he had heard! He would be reminded, and would doubtless cut the thread of life of the two old people. The lady has spoken; it was an indiscretion. What can the duke do? Shall he speak also? Certainly not. He merely makes a gesture, an eloquent gesture, which speaks. With great emotion, he raises his finger quickly, and lays it across his mouth, and then turns the open hand towards the lady, a little higher than the shoulder, saying, " hush! "

An Englishman cannot teach as you do, monsieur, for the Englishman does not gesticulate, nor the American either. — I beg your pardon, mademoiselle; eloquence calls for gesture. — I have not seen our orators gesticulate. — What! And your prince of orators? — Who, monsieur? — Can you ask me? Mr. Wendell Phillips. — Have you heard him speak? — Yes, and I bless God for it; I had that happiness last evening. — Did he speak yesterday? — Did you not know it? were you not present? — No. — Have you heard his lecture on " The Lost Arts?" — No, never. — I pity you and I blame you. — Why? — What! you are from Athens and you do not go to hear the first of Athenians, speaking on art, on the beautiful; an Athenian that old Athens, the true, the ancient Athens would have cheered. — He is a radical

reformer, monsieur. — Is it always wrong to be radical?
Was he wrong the day on which he attacked slavery at
its root, brave as a hero, heroic as a saint, as an apostle of
truth and justice? — He was beautiful then. — Yes, beautiful as Socrates, beautiful as Washington and Lincoln,
beautiful as Jeanne d'Arc, beautiful as Christopher Colum-
bus, beautiful with daring, with radicalism in his enthusiasm for justice. — You are enthusiastic also, monsieur. —
Thank you. — But he sympathizes with the French social-
ists. Do you sympathize with them too? — Frankly
no. But am I right or wrong? Once more the famous
"*Que sais-je*"? ("What do I know?") of Montaigne, is the
refuge of the wise man. Mr. W. Phillips admires them
and G. Sand does also. I have been struck by the appre-
ciation this great woman has for Louis Blanc, a socialist. —
In which book? — In her celebrated work "*Histoire de ma
Vie.*" — Does she admire Louis Blanc? — Very much.
She has moved me deeply. I ask myself if the great
socialist historian is not the great man of the future. — Do
you believe so? — "*Que sais-je?*" I shall study him
seriously. — What has he written? — He has written a
great deal. He is a philosopher, an historian, a reformer. —
Name his books, if you please. — *L'Histoire de France;
l'Histoire de dix ans; les Lettres sur l'Angleterre.* — Are
these great works? — Do not doubt it. The present and
the future will have to take them into account. — Is it
necessary to read them? — You will see later. There
are so many great French books that the lifetime of a
man is not sufficient for reading them. — With which are
we to commence? — With the greatest; I will name them
to you when the time comes. For the present, listen,
talk, search, do not read, and beware, mademoiselle, of

judging lightly again men like W. Phillips. — I see that I was wrong, monsieur; the Americans are not more obstinate than the French; they yield when one enlightens them with good reasons. But does the prince of our orators, as you call him, gesticulate like the French? — He says nothing, does not speak an instant, without a gesture; and what gestures! At any moment a Greek artist would take him to form a statue. — Has he taste? — The purest taste. I have never heard any thing, or seen any thing, more beautiful. Thought, word, gesture, it is the ideal of eloquence. He has the Greek moderation, the famous "*ni trop ni trop peu*," (the happy medium). Do you prefer him to M. Thiers? — Comparisons are often odious. — Why? — Because they make us look for preferences, and consequently point out faults and spots. It is an unhealthy occupation. — What must we do? — Give yourselves up to admire. It is one of the greatest enjoyments. — But you have said nothing of the forehead. — I promise you to speak of it the next time.

IV.

THE GRAMMAR.

I REPRODUCE here a note from the last chapter but one of the book.

" At the point at which we have arrived, it is not amiss, it is even useful, to study the grammar. I do this in my classes every year the third term. It is one of the most interesting parts of our work, both for my pupils and myself. I see them come to the class, in spite of the heat of June, with a persistency which almost astonishes me, and which I admire; they ask me for a lesson in grammar as one of the greatest of favors. It is easily understood. These dear companions of a year's journeying through France and among the French, are acquainted with our grammar before the day on which we open it. There only remain for us to examine the great questions, the points which are difficult even for the French. It is from that time a work of the intelligence, which is full of serious enjoyment. We do it, besides, in an original manner, and one which is not imagined by the existing grammars. Thus we have studied this year the subjunctive in a volume of G. Sand. This appears strange to persons who are only acquainted with the routine, and who seem to ignore that the works of the masters have preceded grammars, that the epoch which one calls in literature the epoch of grammarians is already an epoch of decadence, because the grammarians soon forget the masters and know only the grammarians whom they study and copy. These people seem to ignore that the grammars come only after the books, as the generalization comes after the facts of observation; and that it is to the books one must resort constantly, since that is the only source.

"It is then only the great writers who can make us comprehend this elegant and incomparable beauty of our language. 'The French,' said to me one day Professor Hadley of Yale, that illustrious *savant* that America has recently lost, 'is perhaps the most beautiful of the living languages, and assuredly the most elegant, thanks to its subjunctive. We English have almost entirely lost ours, and with it the delicate shades of thought.' Well! I defy any teacher to make us realize these shades, this use so delicate of the subjunctive, from the grammars: they know nothing of the niceties of the language. We must learn to feel them, to appreciate them, and to love them from the great masters.

"As for the question of the participle, interminable, almost unintelligible and an affair of memory in the grammars, it has been reduced to *a single rule*, and I have seen my pupils resolve promptly with this one rule, once thoroughly understood, all the cases of the ' *Grammaire des Grammaires*' by Girault-Duvivier. I affirm that the pupils who have understood this rule, employ the participle more correctly, beyond comparison, than the young people of the best colleges and schools of France. For there, one is shamefully ignorant of the participle, because there, as here, one is only acquainted with the absurd and powerless method of the grammars. One does not even consider that man is a being endowed with intelligence, and without ceremony he is treated as a parrot.

"I will give perhaps some time to the public this portion of my teaching; my pupils have frequently urged me to do so this summer, and I can excuse myself for not having fulfilled this duty, only by saying that I am not entirely prepared as yet. Every original and new production demands to be ripened, and requires long study, numerous researches, and serious meditation. When my work is finished, I shall communicate to my colleagues and to the public this crowning-piece of the present work."

Meanwhile, what is to be done, do you say? What grammar must we use at the end of our teaching? You understand very well that I do not recommend to you any.

I have not found a single one which has for our pupils the slightest value, not a single one which is not of a nature to do much harm and no good, not one that my classes consent to use after the course which they have been through. Have they not all the capital fault of speaking English, of teaching French by means of English, the most absurd and the most impossible thing in the world? I have never opened any of them without my good sense revolting, and without evoking the shade of Montaigne to show him where we are after three centuries of progress in every thing.

But what is to be done? First, do not despond, my dear colleagues; when you have arrived with your pupils at this point of our lessons, you and they will share our disgust for grammars written in English. I assure you that you will not open one of them. Your pupils will be already acquainted with the grammar by practice, and will be ready to form with you the rules of the language. If you wish, open in their presence a French grammar of France, which does not know of the existence of English, the smallest you can find, and give yourself the pleasure of proving together that you all know the grammar. They would laugh heartily, these pupils who speak and write French without having heard even the words *French grammar;* who have talked with you during a year on every subject, and exchanged with you in French thousands and thousands of ideas; who are acquainted with the books of Corneille, Molière, Racine, Pascal, La Rochefoucauld, Victor Hugo, George Sand, Guizot, Thiers, and twenty others, — they would laugh heartily, I say, if you wished to teach them that there are three accents in French; that there are only two genders; that a cedilla is put under the ç in certain cases; that our language has no declensions like the Latin; that *dans, de, avec,* etc., are French prepositions; that one must say *l'Amérique,* and not *le Boston,* but simply *Boston* without the article; that *mon, notre, votre* are possessive adjectives; that *qui? que? quoi?* are interrogative pronouns; if you wished to teach them that the verb *aller* is irregular; that we say in the present, *je vais,* in the future, *j'irai,* etc.; that the verb *vouloir* takes no preposition; that we say, *je ne veux pas étudier,* and not, *je ne veux pas d'étudier* or *à étudier une, "French Grammar."*

But there is the grammar. Do you not see that they know it all, and that it only remains for you to examine what the most intelligent men examine everywhere, the great, difficult, and curious questions of the languages?

I ask pardon for this development; I thought it indispensable. I hope also that I have offended no one, for I can declare that I have had in view no grammarian, and wished to strike only at this fundamental error in general, the most detrimental thing in the world to teaching, — a French grammar written in English.[1]

---

[1] It will be understood that the criticism I make on the grammars is not in reference to the teaching of the universities, where it is not the aim to teach the students the spoken language.

V.

CONVERSATION.

VICTOR COUSIN says, "L'art de parler sert beaucoup à l'art d'écrire, néanmoins ce sont deux arts différents ; et pour atteindre la perfection de la conversation écrite, il faudrait joindre, quand on tient la plume, à l'allure naturelle et libre, à l'heureux abandon de la parole, une réflexion prompte et sûre, capable de surveiller l'inspiration sans la gêner, et d'en émonder légèrement le luxe en en conservant l'aisance, la fraîcheur, la fécondité. Enfants de la scolastique, nous dissertons, nous ne causons pas, je veux dire la plume à la main. Seul au printemps de la civili sation antique et dans la fleur du génie grec, Platon a dérobé ce secret à la Muse, et il l'a emporté avec lui."

If one does not converse in books, if Plato alone has been able to do it, at least they converse in the *salons* of France. Conversation is one of the great glories, a *chef-d'œuvre* of French society. In other countries, it has neither been seen nor known at any time. I am not making a digression at this moment; I am keeping closely to my subject, as will be seen presently, when I draw my conclusion.

But first permit me, reader, to show you the queen of conversation, and to gather for that purpose a flower from the garden of a celebrated woman, I mean from "*Le grand Cyrus*" of Mlle de Scudéry. The queen, as you know, is Mme la marquise de Rambouillet.

To her illustrious *hôtel* came every week persons of the highest rank, even princes and princesses; "but *la spiri-tuelle* marquise considered merit more important than birth: she asked not for insignias of nobility from those who sought after her society, and one was courteously received in her *salon*, if one only brought there *esprit* and talent, accompanied by good manners. Everybody gained by this intercourse; the nobility grew polished, and acquired a taste and respect for culture, and men of letters felt their intelligence elevated as well as their manners."

I beg you to note these words, *esprit*, talent and good manners, and to represent them to yourself as being yet living in good French society.

But my lady readers ask me if *la marquise* was beauti-ful, if she had extraordinary charms. I gather in the gar-den of Mlle de Scudéry an answer:

"Je ne vous dis point que vous vous figuriez la beauté que nos peintres donnent à Vénus, pour comprendre la sienne, car elle ne serait pas assez modeste; ni celle de Pallas, parce qu'elle serait trop fière; ni celle de Junon qui ne serait pas assez charmante; ni celle de Diane qui serait un peu trop sauvage; mais je vous dirai que, pour la représenter, il faudrait prendre de toutes les figures qu'on donne à ces déesses ce qu'elles ont de beau, et l'on en ferait peut-être une passable peinture . . . La majesté de toute sa personne est digne d'admiration, et il sort je ne sais quel éclat de ses yeux qui imprime le respect dans l'âme de tous ceux qui la regardent; et pour moi, je vous avoue que je n'ai jamais pu l'approcher sans sentir dans mon cœur je ne sais quelle crainte respectueuse, qui m'a obligée de songer plus à moi, étant auprès d'elle, qu'en au-cun autre lieu du monde où j'ai jamais été . . . Si on voulait donner un corps à la Gloire pour la faire aimer par tout le monde, je voudrais faire sa peinture, et, si l'on en donnait un à la Vertu, je voudrais aussi la représenter . . . Simple et sans pédanterie, accueillante pour tout le monde, sans humeur, sans caprice et toujours la même, elle avait beaucoup d'esprit naturel, une culture très-variée, de rares connaissances en toutes choses, une grande lecture dans les littératures italienne et espagnole, sans parler des qualités de son âme, la modestie, le désintéressement, la bonté, la constance en tous ses attachements . . . Elle connaît tous les grands ouvrages en prose et en vers ; elle en juge pourtant avec une modération merveilleuse, ne quittant jamais la bienséance de son sexe. Il n'y a personne en toute la cour, qui ait quelque esprit et quelque vertu, qui n'aille chez elle. Rien n'est trouvé beau, si elle ne l'a approuvé ; il ne vient pas même un étranger à Paris qu'il ne veuille la voir et lui rendre hommage."

Is this not indeed the queen of society and of conversation, and do you know another woman in the world who has exercised a like power ? To pass one evening in her *salon*, would you not, lady readers, go to the end of the world, and back to the time of Richelieu ? Before the queen and conversing with her and her company, you would see the great Condé, his sister Mme la duchesse de Longueville, the celebrated marquise de Sévigné, Mme de La Fayette, Corneille, and Bossuet. There is the origin and the flower of conversation in France. The marquise de Rambouillet is dead, but she has left a whole world of sons and daughters. This world is in France in the highest and most cultivated society. And it is only there. These people converse with an ease and a charm on all subjects, the greatest as the most simple ; and there is there an exchange of ideas on a thousand questions, a fund of information acquired without effort, which is absolutely ignored outside of France.

Here I am at my conclusion. Can a foreigner learn the French language, become French, for he must become French to know the language, can he do it by means of grammars and dictionaries? — will he find there the palest ray only of this light, so soft and so beautiful, which shines in the *salon* of Mme de Rambouillet and in French society? It is almost ridiculous even to put the question. It is necessary then to converse; you see very well, to learn French, pupils must resort to conversation, and nothing else.

Also on all sides are advertised courses of conversation; and books of conversation for the Americans have even been published sometimes. But there are conversations — and conversations, as there is language — and language. Whatever the conversation where you learn to speak, such will be your language. Beware of it! There is the language of the peasant, the language of the shopkeeper, the language of a cultivated and educated society — these are three different languages: there is even the language of your dress-maker. Choose that which suits you, and, I beg you, take the richest.

You know that the English dictionary has as many as one hundred thousand words, according to certain authorities. Max Müller says in one of his Oxford lectures that certain English peasants have less than three hundred words in their vocabulary. He continues, " A well-educated man in England, who has been at the university, who reads his Bible, his Shakspeare and the 'Times,' seldom uses more than about three or four thousand words in actual conversation. . . . Eloquent speakers may rise to a command of ten thousand words. Shakspeare, the richest poet in the world, has employed fifteen thousand words. There are eight thousand in Milton, and five thousand six hundred and forty-two in the Old Testament." What is true of the English is true also of the French. There are a thousand different languages in all the civilized countries, for the words correspond to the head, to the ideas of each person; as many ideas as we have, just so many words we need to clothe them. Do you not see that here is a consequence of these premises! You, who are studying French, need a person to teach it to you, who has at least as many ideas as you. If not, your teacher will not give you a language sufficient to express your ideas; in English you may be an intelligent and educated person, but in French you will be a poor, stupid creature, who can speak of nothing but the rain and the beautiful weather, of cauliflowers and green pease, of a concert perhaps, and of a dress. I have seen such persons, intelligent in their own language, but incapable of approaching a serious or elevated idea in mine, and I knew what course of French conversation these persons had pursued. Is then a talk like the following the image of the society of Rambouillet and of our present select society? "Good morning, madame. — *Je vous salue, monsieur.* — Did you go to the concert yesterday? — Yes, it was delightful. — Were there many people there? — Oh, yes! the hall was very crowded. — Madame Lucca sang well? — Like an angel; she had on a beautiful pink dress which was exceedingly becoming to her, and do you know that Mr. X. has sent her a superb bouquet?"

It does you no harm, madame, to hold this conversation

with your teacher, but do not pass all your time on it, and mount a little higher, you who have a head so well informed, and who would say so well in French a thousand things that one would be happy to hear from you.

Unfortunately, the books of conversation that have been put thus far into the hands of pupils are as destitute of ideas, as empty as the dialogue that I have presented above. It is truly deplorable, and I do not know how the committees of schools understand their grave mission. Are they not then conscious of their responsibility? If they do not know the French language, are they the less excusable for not addressing themselves to competent men? Would the learned professors of Harvard and of Yale, for example, refuse them some good advice? I am sure they would not, and I am persuaded that not one of them would give his approbation to the employment of these manuals.

Why then are all these books so poor? The reason for it is still in the great defect, the teaching by grammars and dictionaries. One looks only for words and thinks only of teaching words. One has no ideas and attaches no price to ideas, and yet ideas alone can lead to the knowledge even of words. I will be more explicit in relating a fact of my experience.

While at New Haven, I taught a select class formed of the tutors of Yale, during four months and a half. They spent two hours with me five times a week. After this time they were almost as French as I, and I have afterwards passed with them more than one evening without hearing a word of English pronounced. The conversation was so animated and so interesting that I believed myself in the midst of a select club of France. I never taught words to these gentlemen, I only took care to communicate to them my ideas and to receive theirs: after a month's time their ear was accustomed to the sounds of the language, and we discussed a tragedy of Sophocles, or of Æschylus, or of Euripides, of Racine, or of Shakspeare; we talked about France, England, America; reasoned upon an Oration of Cicero, upon Bacon or La Rochefoucauld, upon men and things; one of my pupils who was studying philosophy deeply, spoke to us of John Stuart Mill and of the contemporaneous philosophers of England; we conversed about Renan and Littré; another of my pupils who had been an officer in the civil war related to us his experience; a third made me acquainted with the different churches of this country, etc. This is not a hundredth part of our conversations. I would forget that I was teaching and they would forget that they were studying French: they have told me so many times. And yet they were studying it admirably, since they said nothing in English, and since, after four months and a half, the acquisition of the language was made for ever.

Is it not clear then, that the means of learning the words of a language, is to not think about them, but to produce ideas constantly, using for instrument only words of the language one is studying? I defy any thoughtful man to gainsay me.

Thus you see, it is the forgetfulness of ideas, caused by the error of the method, which puts on the school programme the most miserable text-books. And the evil goes still farther, for this same defect also causes books to be given to the pupils to read, which are chosen without discrimination, the most wretched productions of France, that no intelligent man reads in that country, or at best a few little dramas which have had in France only the success of a moment. I have read from six to eight thousand volumes in my language, and I know the opinion of good judges on as many others, and I have found in America, on the programme of schools which have only two or three books, works of whose existence I was not aware, so unknown are they to the literary men of France. Is this not shameful for your country? I have heard also more than one person tell me that they did not know what to read, that there was nothing to read in French, in that language which has the richest and the greatest literature of modern times. Is not that still more shameful for you and for those who have directed you in your reading? I recommend to the reader the forty-ninth and last chapter of my work on " The books to read." It examines the great books and presents a choice library for all those who read.

The best book to use in schools is the volume of Fables of La Fontaine. These fables furnish to the teacher an inexhaustible source of conversation on all subjects in the world, and are clothed in the most delightful of poetry. It is unpardonable to employ any other book in teaching, if one has not at the same time La Fontaine. I refer my reader to the two chapters on La Fontaine in my book, and also to the nine or ten fables which I study there. He will see what is the value of La Fontaine, and how he must be understood and presented to the pupils, making the fable examined prolific by the calling up of numerous thoughts which these fables inspire.

To aid those of my colleagues who will practise the system of teaching without grammar, I shall publish next year a course on La Fontaine. The volume will comprise about fifty fables, studied as are those which are in the work that I present to the public to-day. I have the conviction that the method will be adopted everywhere, because it is the only good one, and that it will be necessary to acknowledge it. But as it is a radical revolution in teaching, I know that it is desirable to lead thither the new-comers. It is for this reason that I have decided to put a La Fontaine by the side of the present volume.

I close this work here. I shall always be happy to assist with advice from my experience those of my colleagues who will do me the honor to ask it of me. For the present I lay aside the pen, but I shall resume it. It is only after long hesitation and after much actual experience, that I have conceived the resolution of publishing my views. I am decided now to maintain them to the final triumph.

These pages are followed by a few chapters extracted from the book, " *Causeries avec mes élèves,*" and by the analytical table of the work. This table shows better than any explanation the wealth of ideas that there is in an actual conversation. However, the book represents only a very slight portion of the talks I have had with my pupils; twenty volumes would be needed to present to the public, even in succinct, the ideas that we agitate together, and the vast vocabulary that we need to express them.

One final remark with regard to the table. Like every table, and less than any other, since it is the table of a conversation, it does not show the connection of ideas. This connection exists in the book from the first word to the very last. It is in every thing the faithful image of a conversation, where a delicate and almost imperceptible thread leads all the discourse. A conversation, — such is the character and the value of the book. No other resembles it. If a written conversation existed which deserved this name, I would not have given this one to the public.

VI.

FOUR CHAPTERS FROM "CAUSERIES AVEC MES ÉLÈVES."

CHAP. X. — LES OREILLES. — LES ÉCOUTEURS.

Revenons aux parties du corps.

Nous avons deux oreilles, une de chaque côté de la tête. L'oreille est l'organe de l'ouïe. Entendez-vous ? — Oui, j'entends. — C'est un grand bonheur d'entendre. Le sourd n'entend pas, il est misérable. Est-il malheureux ? — Je ne sais pas. — C'est bien. Les misérables ne sont pas nécessairement malheureux. — Le vieillard entend-il ? — Oui, plus ou moins ; il y a des vieillards qui sont presque sourds. Il y en a qui sont tout-à-fait sourds.

Voilà un chien sur ce tableau. Voyez-vous ses oreilles ? Entend-il aussi bien que l'homme ? — Il entend mieux que l'homme. — Il a l'ouïe extrêmement fine. Pouvez-vous agiter les oreilles ? — Non. — Le chien les agite, et quand il écoute, il les dresse. Le cheval aussi. Dresser est synonyme de lever. .... Ne vous appuyez pas comme cela, mon ami, la main sur l'oreille. Pourquoi bouchez-vous une de vos oreilles ? Voyez, monsieur, il m'écoute des deux oreilles pour comprendre mieux ce que je dis.

Prêtez-moi votre oreille, car je parle à votre oreille pour vous donner ma langue.

Les livres s'adressent-ils à votre oreille?—Non.—Eh bien! ne vous adressez pas à eux non plus. Quand votre oreille sera française, à la bonne heure! Vous ouvrirez les livres alors pour mettre beaucoup de mots dans votre vocabulaire, et de la variété, de la richesse dans votre conversation, et aussi pour mettre des connaissances, des idées dans votre tête.—Ouvrirons-nous la grammaire, monsieur?—Pourquoi non? Quand le moment sera venu, nous l'étudierons profondément.—La grammaire est-elle bête?—Oh! que non. Elle nous inspire la plus grande admiration, quand nous la comprenons.—Faut-il commencer ou finir par la grammaire?—Vous voyez bien que nous ne commençons pas par la grammaire, et cependant vous me comprenez. Commencez par former votre oreille en écoutant, et votre langue en parlant.—Et puis que ferons-nous?—Vous ouvrirez les livres des grands écrivains.—Les comprendrons-nous?—Sans doute; quand vous comprendrez mes paroles, quand vous parlerez un peu, nous prendrons un livre, et vous le comprendrez.—Et après, que ferons-nous?—Vous êtes bien curieuse aujourd'hui, madame.

Votre voisin n'est-il pas curieux? On dit que les femmes sont plus curieuses que les hommes. Est-ce vrai?—Je ne le crois pas du tout. Je connais des hommes très-curieux.—Je n'en doute pas, madame. Connaissez-vous le duc de Saint-Simon?—Oui, j'ai lu ses fameux *Mémoires* en anglais. J'espère les lire un jour en français. Il est curieux, n'est-ce pas?—Oui, plus curieux qu'aucune femme. La curiosité est-elle un défaut?—Pas toujours, c'est souvent une qualité.—Oui, cela dépend de l'objet. Il y a curiosité et curiosité, comme on dit. Mais pourquoi ne parlons-nous pas de l'oreille ?

Entendons-nous aussi bien de l'oreille gauche que de l'oreille droite ? — Généralement oui. — Il n'y a pas de différence entre les deux oreilles. L'une est aussi bonne que l'autre. Cependant la main droite n'est-elle pas plus forte que la main gauche ? — C'est une tout autre affaire. Nous exerçons la main droite plus que l'autre, mais nous exerçons les deux oreilles également. — Avez-vous lu Molière, monsieur ? — Un peu, en traduction. — Il y a dans une comédie de Molière un personnage qui dit à son interlocuteur : "Passez de l'autre côté, car cette oreille-ci est destinée pour les langues étrangères ; l'autre est pour la langue maternelle." Je suppose, mon ami, que vous ne ressemblez pas à cet original. Ne bouchez donc plus votre oreille droite, ni la gauche non plus. Le français les réclame toutes deux.

Voilà la partie externe de l'oreille : c'est le pavillon ; voilà le trou, voilà le bout de l'oreille. Aimez-vous les petites oreilles, les trouvez-vous jolies ? — Je les préfère beaucoup aux oreilles d'âne. — Oh ! celles-là sont laides. Je soupçonne l'âne de ne pas écouter, quand on lui parle. Il fait la sourde oreille, c'est-à-dire il ne veut pas écouter. Il est obstiné, têtu, indocile, et aussi stupide, dit-on. C'est sa réputation.

Suffit-il d'entendre pour comprendre ? — Non. — Que faut-il de plus ? — Il faut écouter. — Ah ! voilà. Ce n'est pas tout d'entendre, il faut écouter. C'est une grande qualité que de savoir écouter. Combien peu d'hommes savent écouter ! Pour un orateur, un bon écouteur est un trésor. Méré dit : " Les bons écouteurs font les bons parleurs." Comprenez-vous cela ? — Oui, je comprends les mots, mais je ne saisis pas bien la pensée. — Ce n'est pas difficile. Voyons. Quand vous parlez, si votre auditeur est distrait, s'il n'écoute pas, n'êtes-vous pas distrait vous-même par sa distraction et découragé ? — Oh ! oui, monsieur. — Pouvez-vous être éloquent alors, n'êtes-vous pas froid et sans inspiration ? — Si. — Quand M. Thiers parle à la tribune française, un silence religieux règne dans la chambre ; il a sept cents écouteurs qui l'inspirent ; il a toutes les oreilles pour sa parole. Mais quelle parole ! quelle clarté ! quelle lumière il jette sur toute question politique, financière, économique, n'importe !

Lisez-vous quelquefois la feuille nommée " *The Nation ?* " — Oui, toutes les semaines. — Vous faites bien. C'est la grande feuille américaine. Ne se trompe-t-elle jamais ? — Si fait, monsieur ; Dieu seul est infaillible. — Avez-vous lu un article dans cette publication hebdomadaire, qui prétend que le français n'a pas de mot qui corresponde au terme anglais *listener ?* — Oui, je ne l'ai pas oublié. — Avez-vous cru cela ? — Sans doute. — Le croyez-vous encore ? — Je ne le crois plus du tout. — J'en suis bien aise. Car un mot n'est pas peu de chose, et celui d'écouteur est plein de signification, n'est-ce pas ? — Oui, oui, monsieur ? — Du reste, voyez les conséquences. Les bons écouteurs font les bons parleurs, n'est-ce pas ? — Oui, c'est la pensée de Méré. — Pas d'écouteurs, pas de parleurs ; n'est-ce pas une conséquence de cette pensée ? — C'est clair. — Donc s'il n'y a pas d'écouteurs en France, il n'y a pas de parleurs, du moins pas de bons parleurs, pas de grands orateurs. La conclusion est-elle juste ? — Oui. — Bossuet, Bourdaloue, Mirabeau, Berryer, M. Guizot, M. Thiers, et cent autres, sont comme des faits qui protestent. Les faits n'ont jamais tort. Une nation qui parle bien, une nation éloquente, a toujours des écouteurs, de bons écouteurs ; c'est une part de son inspiration.

Y a-t-il beaucoup de préjugés dans le monde, madame ? — Helas ! oui. — Les Français sont-ils légers ? — C'est l'opinion générale en Angleterre. — Oui, et les Anglais l'ont importée en Amérique. C'est le contraire qui est vrai, mesdames.

Il est onze heures, nous devons nous séparer. Je n'ai pas le temps de discuter ce misérable préjugé. Quand vous serez chez vous, prenez *Aurora Leigh* et lisez-en le 6ᵉ chant, si je ne me trompe. C'est le chant qui commence ainsi : —

> " The English have a scornful insular way
> Of calling the French light. The levity
> Is in the judgment only, which yet stands ;
> For say a foolish thing but oft enough
> And " . . .

Adieu, mesdames.

Questions. — Où sont les oreilles ? — Quel est l'organe de l'ouïe ? — Est-il plus triste de ne pas entendre que de ne pas voir ? — Comment appelle-t-on l'homme qui n'entend pas ? — Ne le plaignez-vous pas ? — Est-ce que le sourd peut parler ? — Entendez-vous ? — Entendez-vous la nuit, quand vous dormez ? — N'entendez-vous pas, pendant le sommeil, quand on frappe fortement sur votre porte ? — Etes-vous complètement sourd la nuit ? — Est-ce que l'âge affaiblit ou fortifie l'organe de l'ouïe ? — Le vieillard n'a-t-il pas l'oreille dure ? — Est-ce que le chien a l'oreille dure ou fine ? — L'a-t-il plus fine ou moins fine que l'homme ?

Suffit-il d'entendre pour comprendre ? ne faut-il pas écouter ? — Quand vous bouchez vos oreilles, entendez-vous ? — Est-il bon d'écouter ? — Est-il beau d'écouter aux portes ? — Est-ce une bonne ou une mauvaise curiosité ?

Apprend-on une langue par les yeux ou par les oreilles ? — Est-ce par les yeux que les enfants apprennent la langue de leur mère ? — Les livres s'adressent-ils aux yeux ou aux oreilles ? — Faut-il lire les livres ou écouter la parole humaine pour apprendre à parler ?

Aimez-vous la grammaire ? — Est-ce que l'étude de la grammaire est facile ? — Les enfants comprennent-ils la grammaire ? — Petit ami, comprenez-vous la grammaire anglaise ? — Quand on étudie la grammaire, faut-il l'étudier avec la mémoire ou avec le jugement ? — Est-ce qu'un perroquet peut apprendre à réciter une règle de grammaire ? — Peut-il arriver à la comprendre ? — De ces deux travaux, réciter la grammaire et comprendre la grammaire, lequel est le travail d'homme, et lequel est le travail de perroquet ? — Le perroquet est-il curieux ? — Et la femme ? — Et l'homme ? — Lequel est le plus curieux des trois ? — Lequel est le moins curieux des trois ? — Est-ce que cette question est facile à décider ? — Ne pensez-vous pas que le perroquet n'est pas moins curieux que la femme ? — Et le duc de Saint-Simon ? — Est-il mauvais d'être curieux ?

Expliquez pourquoi on entend aussi bien d'une oreille que de l'autre ? — Entend-on aussi bien d'une oreille que des deux oreilles ? — Avez-vous une oreille pour le français et une pour l'anglais ?

Qui est Molière ? — Qui est monsieur Thiers ? — Lequel est le plus grand des deux ? — Est-ce que la feuille " *The Nation* " est infaillible ? — Est-ce un journal proprement dit ou une feuille hebdomadaire ?

Quelle heure est-il ? Est-ce que votre montre est bonne ?
— Va-t-elle ? — N'avance-t-elle pas ? — Que faites-vous
quand elle retarde ?

CHAP. XV. — LE BOUC ET LE RENARD.

JE vous salue, mesdames, et je vous donne tout de suite
la fable promise.   Mais elle est difficile ; je crains que vous
ne la compreniez pas sans explication.   Je vais vous la
raconter en prose avant de la lire.

" Le renard et le bouc étaient ensemble en voyage.   Ils
allaient de compagnie.   Le voyage fut agréable, et je suis
bien sûr que le renard fit beaucoup rire le bouc.   C'est un
personnage spirituel, qui a toujours à sa disposition quelque
histoire amusante et quelques bons mots pour égayer la compagnie.   Mais il est trompeur, il abuse de la supériorité de
son esprit, et il faut se défier de lui.   Il est passé maître en fait
de tromperie, dit La Fontaine.   Et en cette circonstance
il aura beau jeu, car son compagnon est une véritable ga-
nache, comme disait Napoléon de l'empereur d'Autriche ;
il ne voyait pas plus loin que son nez.

Après avoir beaucoup marché, beaucoup causé, beaucoup
ri, les deux compagnons eurent soif.   Heureusement pour
eux, ils rencontrèrent un puits, et altérés, comme ils étaient, ils n'hésitèrent pas à descendre pour boire.   Ils
burent et ils burent abondamment.   Alors seulement
ils songèrent à sortir du puits.   Probablement le renard
y avait pensé auparavant, car je ne puis croire qu'un animal aussi intelligent que celui-là descende dans un puits
sans savoir d'avance comment il en sortira.   Mais bien
sûr, le bouc n'y avait pas pensé.   Aussi vous allez voir
comment il fut joué par le renard.   Que fait celui-ci ?   Il

va tout simplement employer le bouc comme une échelle.
Il lui dit: " Mon cher ami, j'ai un moyen de sortir du
puits : tu mettras tes pieds de devant contre le mur, et tu
lèveras tes cornes en haut ; je grimperai le long de ton
échine, et puis je sauterai sur tes cornes, et de là au bord
du puits. Quand je serai sauvé, je te tirerai dehors."
Voilà le bouc qui joue le rôle d'une vraie machine. Le
renard est bientôt sur le bord du puits. Une fois là,
trompeur comme il est, il ne fait rien pour le bouc, et bien
plus il se moque de lui, lui reproche sa bêtise et sa cré-
dulité. Il l'exhorte ironiquement à la patience. " Si tu
avais, dit-il, autant d'esprit que de barbe au menton, tu ne
serais pas descendu dans ce puits. Adieu, j'ai une affaire
qui me presse ; je n'ai pas le temps de m'arrêter da-
vantage."

Voici la morale: en toute chose, il faut considérer la fin.
En d'autres termes : n'entreprenez pas une affaire sans
savoir comment vous la terminerez. Ecoutons les vers de
La Fontaine.

Capitaine renard allait de compagnie
Avec son ami bouc des plus haut encornés :
Celui-ci ne voyait pas plus loin que son nez,
L'autre était passé maître en fait de tromperie.
La soif les obligea de descendre en un puits ;
　　Là, chacun d'eux se désaltère.
Après qu'abondamment tous deux en eurent pris,
Le renard dit au bouc : Que ferons-nous, compère ?
Ce n'est pas tout de boire, il faut sortir d'ici.
Lève tes pieds en haut, et tes cornes aussi ;
Mets-les contre le mur ; le long de ton échine
　　Je grimperai premièrement ;
　　Puis sur tes cornes m'élevant,
　　A l'aide de cette machine,

> De ce lieu-ci je sortirai,
>   Après quoi je t'en tirerai.
> Par ma barbe ! dit l'autre, il est bon ; et je loue
>   Les gens bien sensés comme toi.
>   Je n'aurais jamais, quant à moi,
>   Trouvé ce secret, je l'avoue.
> Le renard sort du puits, laisse son compagnon,
>   Et vous lui fait un beau sermon
>   Pour l'exhorter à patience.
> Si le ciel t'eût, dit-il, donné par excellence
> Autant de jugement que de barbe au menton,
>   Tu n'aurais pas, à la légère,
> Descendu dans ce puits.   Or, adieu ; j'en suis hors :
> Tâche de t'en tirer, et fais tous tes efforts ;
>   Car, pour moi, j'ai certaine affaire
> Qui ne me permet pas d'arrêter en chemin.
> En toute chose il faut considérer la fin.

Avez-vous compris la fable ? — Oui, mais nous comprenons mieux votre prose que les vers de La Fontaine. — Je n'en doute point. — Si vous aviez commencé par les vers, nous n'aurions rien compris. — Non. — Pourquoi le poëte appelle-t-il le renard *capitaine* ? — C'est un véritable capitaine. Il a l'habitude de conduire les autres ; il est toujours le chef de sa compagnie. — *Son ami bouc*, dit-il ; est-il vraiment l'ami du bouc ? — Il y a si peu d'amis dans le monde ! l'amitié véritable rend les amis célèbres dans l'histoire. — C'est vrai. — En connaissez-vous ? — Oui, monsieur, la sœur de mademoiselle. — Oh oui ! certes : je pensais que vous l'aviez oubliée. — Elle était à New York ; je ne pouvais pas lui parler de nos leçons. — Demandez-lui, cher ami, quelles sont les amitiés célèbres. — Je les connais : Don Quichotte et Dulcinée, Castor et Pollux. — Pardon ! Dulcinée était l'amour du chevalier de la Manche. — Quelle différence y a-t-il entre l'amitié et l'amour ? —

Que vous êtes curieux ! Victoria avait de l'amour pour le prince Albert, Castor avait de l'amitié pour Pollux. Ne connaissez-vous pas d'autres amis dans l'histoire, mesdames ? — Oui, Oreste et Pylade, Achille et Patrocle, Nisus et Euryale. — Où avez-vous vu Nisus et Euryale ? — C'est un épisode de Virgile que j'ai traduit à *Vassar College.* — Il est touchant, n'est-ce pas, madame ? — Oui, je l'aime beaucoup ; mon professeur m'a dit que Virgile est plus tendre qu'Homère. — Que sais-je ? Homère a Andromaque et Hector, Achille et Patrocle, Ulysse et Pénélope. — Mais on dit le tendre Virgile. — Vous avez raison, il a fait Didon. — Est-il aussi grand qu'Homère ? — Non, non, madame ; il a imité le poëte grec avec beaucoup d'art, voilà tout. Il avait le goût délicat et une douce poésie dans son âme. Mais le chant spontané, la grande inspiration, la vérité, la nature, la foi, tout cela ne s'imite pas. Marchons tous après Homère dans notre petit bout de chemin, mesdames. Soyons nous-mêmes, chantons ou disons notre propre âme et nos propres idées. — Vous n'aimez pas Virgile ? — Je l'aime dans les Eglogues, les Géorgiques, et aux 4° et 9° chants de l'Enéide, j'aime l'amour de Didon et l'amitié de Nisus et Euryale.

Vous n'avez pas dit si le renard était l'ami du bouc ? — Pour sentir l'amitié, il faut être bon, dévoué, se sacrifier au bonheur de ceux qu'on aime, partager leurs peines et leurs plaisirs. Eh bien ! le renard avait-il de l'amitié ? — Non, sans doute : La Fontaine a fait une faute de dire son ami bouc. — Non, il a parlé la langue de tous, qui profane le nom d'ami. Il a fait comme Philinte. — Qui est Philinte ? — Vous le connaîtrez quand vous lirez le Misanthrope de Molière, la plus haute des comédies. Continuez vos questions. — Que signifie *encorné ?* — M. Littré définit

encorné et *cornu* de la même manière : qui a des cornes. —
N'y a-t-il pas de différence ? — Je vous le dirai l'année
prochaine, à notre cours de littérature et de grammaire. — Qu'est-ce que *compère ?* — C'est un nom familier
que l'on donne à son camarade. — Et l'*échine ?* — Regardez le cheval que je vous montre ; voilà l'échine. —
Le bouc était-il une machine ? — Oui, pour le renard. —
Le renard est de l'école de Descartes, monsieur. — Vous
avez raison, mademoiselle. — Que signifie *à la légère ?* —
Sans réflexion. Pensons toujours aux conséquences de
nos actes avant de les poser, et aussi aux conséquences de
nos paroles avant de parler. Celui qui ne parle ni n'agit
jamais à la légère est un sage. Qui est cet homme ! Où
est-il !

CHAP. XXII. — LES YEUX. — ŒDIPE.

Je vais vous interroger sur les yeux, mesdames. Si
vous êtes bien attentives, vous répondrez à toutes les questions sans peine : je les enchaînerai et vous conduirai de
l'une à l'autre.

Voyez-vous ? — Les animaux voient-ils ? — Tous ? —
Le hibou voit-il ? — Voit-il mieux le jour que la nuit ? —
Et la chouette ? — Et le chat-huant ? — Et votre chat,
madame ?

La taupe voit-elle ? — A-t-elle des yeux ? — Aime-t-elle
la lumière ? — Et vous ? — Aimez-vous les oiseaux des
ténèbres ? — Aimez-vous les hommes-hiboux ? — Et les
hommes-taupes ?

Le sphynx a-t-il une bonne vue ? — Aussi bonne que la
nôtre ? — Et l'aigle ? — Napoléon avait-il un œil d'aigle ? —
Et le cardinal de Richelieu ? — Et le comte Cavour ? —
L'aigle voit-il loin ? — Le sphynx a-t-il la vue perçante ?

— Voit-il loin ? — Quelle différence y a-t-il entre l'homme qui a un œil d'aigle et celui qui a un œil de sphynx ? — Lequel des deux enviez-vous le plus ?

Le vieillard a-t-il d'aussi bons yeux que le jeune homme ? — Pourquoi non ? — Le myope voit-il de loin ? — Comment tient-il son livre pour lire ? — Et le vieillard ? — A quoi lui servent les lunettes ? — Pourquoi portez-vous des lunettes, madame ? — Y a-t-il plus de lunettes en Amérique qu'en Europe ? — Pourquoi ?

L'aveugle voit-il ? — Et le borgne ? — Et le louche ? — Quel est le plus à plaindre des trois ? — Connaissez-vous une infirmité humaine plus grande que la cécité ? — N'y a-t-il pas aussi une cécité intellectuelle ? — Peut-on la guérir ? — Comment ?

N'admirez-vous pas le chien de l'aveugle ? — Mon ami, ne vous mettez-vous pas de côté pour laisser passer le chien de l'aveugle ? — Quel sentiment éprouvez-vous dans votre cœur quand vous voyez cet animal conduire cet homme ?

Connaissez-vous le vieil Œdipe ? — Et sa fille Antigone ? — Le vieillard était-il aveugle ? — Aveugle de naissance ? — Qui lui arracha les yeux ? — Etait-il conduit par un chien ou par sa fille ? — N'êtes-vous pas touché de le voir errant loin de sa patrie, appuyé sur le bras d'Antigone, et de lui entendre dire : "Ma fille, tes yeux voient pour toi et pour moi ?" — Désirez-vous entendre parler Œdipe exilé et errant ? — Ecoutez.

ŒDIPE. — "Fille d'un vieillard aveugle, Antigone, en quelle contrée, en quelle ville sommes-nous arrivés ? Qui accueillera aujourd'hui avec une chétive aumône, Œdipe errant ? Il demande peu, il obtient moins encore, et ce peu lui suffit, car les souffrances, la vieillesse, et enfin mon courage m'enseignent la résignation. Mais ma fille, si tu apperçois quelque siége dans un lieu profane, ou dans quelque bois sacré, conduis-moi, et arrêtes-y mes pas, afin de nous informer des lieux où nous sommes. Etrangers en ce pays, nous devons apprendre des habitants ce qu'il convient de faire, et l'accomplir.

ANTIGONE. — Œdipe, père infortuné, je vois dans le lointain les tours, qui entourent la ville. Le lieu où nous sommes est sacré autant que mes yeux peuvent en juger, car il est parsemé de lauriers, d'oliviers, de vignes abondantes, et, sous le feuillage, de nombreux rossignols font entendre leurs chants mélodieux. Repose tes membres sur cette roche grossière, car tu as fait un long chemin, pour un vieillard.

ŒDIPE. — Assieds-moi maintenant, et garde ton père aveugle.

N'êtes-vous pas émus ? — Ne sentez-vous pas le parfum attique ? — Avez-vous jamais senti ce parfum dans Shakspeare ? — Quel spectacle préférez-vous, celui que présente Antigone auprès d'Œdipe, ou le fou auprès du roi Lear ? — Ne sont-ce pas deux grands spectacles ?

Suivrez-vous mon conseil, si je vous recommande de lire cet Œdipe à Colonne, dont les premières lignes ont fait venir les larmes dans vos yeux ? — Ne désirez-vous pas connaître Sophocle, son auteur ?

Voit-on mieux avec deux yeux qu'avec un œil ? — De combien ? — Ne savez-vous pas que Buffon dit d'un treizième. — Est-ce beaucoup ?

Les yeux du louche ont-ils la même direction ? — N'y a-t-il pas des caractères louches ? — Qu'en pensez-vous ? — Ne préférez-vous pas une âme droite ?

Les yeux parlent-ils ? — Que disent-ils ? — Savez-vous lire l'âme dans les yeux ? — Les yeux du bœuf parlent-ils ? — Quels yeux préférez-vous, les yeux de bœuf de Junon ou les yeux couleur de mer de Vénus ?

Nos yeux ne sont-ils pas souvent aveugles pour nous-mêmes ? — Pourquoi ? — Pouvons-nous échapper à l'œil de Dieu ? — N'est-il pas bon de penser que l'œil de Dieu est toujours sur nous ? — Pourquoi ?

CHAP. XXIII. — UNE ANECDOTE. — LE CAUCHEMAR.

Bonjour, mesdames; bonjour, mon ami. Vous avez les yeux gros; avez-vous pleuré. — Oui, monsieur. — Est-ce un méchant garçon qui vous a fait pleurer ? — Non, je ne pleure pas pour si peu; c'est la sœur de mademoiselle. — Est-ce possible ? A-t-elle été méchante pour vous ? — Non, non; elle n'est jamais méchante, mais j'ai rêvé la nuit. — Un mauvais rêve de votre amie. C'est triste; mais n'y pensez pas; votre rêve vous trompe. Vous avez eu peut-être un cauchemar. — Qu'est-ce qu'un cauchemar ? — C'est comme un horrible rêve, un poids incommode qui pèse sur nous pendant le sommeil et nous empêche de nous mouvoir, de parler, de respirer.

Je vais vous dire une anecdote à ce sujet, ou plutôt une histoire vraie. — Nous écoutons de toutes nos oreilles. — Cette histoire nous a été racontée l'année dernière, dans la classe, par un de mes élèves. — Qui est-ce ? — Vous êtes toujours curieuse, petite fille. — Pas plus que George. — C'est vrai; mais George a deux curiosités à satisfaire, la sienne, et . . . — Oh ! monsieur, vous voulez dire la sœur de mademoiselle ; elle n'est pas curieuse autant que Louise, et que toutes les dames qui sont ici. Si vous la connaissiez ! — J'espère que vous me présenterez à elle, et je sais qu'elle est parfaite; calmez-vous, et écoutez l'histoire du cauchemar. Vous la direz ce soir à votre charmante amie. — J'écoute pour nous deux. — A la bonne heure ! — C'est un jeune homme qui parle; il est en ce moment étudiant à Harvard.

"Il faut savoir que je dors avec mon frère. Tous les soirs quand nous allions nous coucher, il devenait triste, inquiet : il avait peur de se mettre au lit. ' Ce maudit cauchemar, me dit-il un jour, me rendra fou. Il vient presque toutes les nuits et je n'ose dormir. — Tu es un poltron. — Que n'es-tu à ma place, une nuit seulement, tu ne serais pas plus brave que moi. C'est terrible; mes cheveux se dressent sur ma tête rien que d'y penser. — Mets un bonnet de nuit. — Ne badine pas, je t'en prie. Imagine-toi un affreux vieillard, avec une figure comme Brigham Young, qui vient se coucher sur moi, pesant comme une montagne, et tenant fixés sur moi des yeux horribles ! — Eh bien ! donne-lui un bon coup de poing sur la tête, au moment où il te lâche. — Tu as peut-être raison.' — Après cette conversation, nous nous mettons au lit. Je m'endors bientôt, mon frère aussi. Au milieu de la nuit, un cri qui fait trembler les vitres de la chambre me tire brusquement de mon sommeil. Mon frère était sur son séant et j'entendais battre son cœur. — ' Que fais-tu ? Qu'y a-t-il ? — C'est le cauchemar. — L'as-tu tué. — Je l'ai manqué ; il était là assis sur mes genoux ; je lui ai lancé mon poing : il était parti. — Laisse-moi dormir, et ne le manque plus, s'il revient. — Non, je te jure ; je me sens du courage.'

J'étais à peine rentré dans mon sommeil que je crie à mon tour, éveillé par la douleur de mon front ; j'avais des tourbillons devant les yeux ; et j'entendais mon frère crier avec enthousiasme en sautant sur son lit : ' Victoire ! victoire ! je ne t'ai pas manqué cette fois, tu ne reviendras plus, misérable, hideux monstre. Victoire ! mon frère, victoire ! — Suis-je donc ton cauchemar ? allume vite la bougie, et viens voir ce que tu as fait de mon front. — Il

était sur mon épaule; il ne reviendra plus! victoire!—
N'entends-tu pas? donne-moi de l'eau et ne tue plus tes
cauchemars. — Hélas! je l'ai manqué.' — Cela peut pa-
raître étrange, mais depuis ce jour mon frère n'a plus eu de
cauchemar. C'est sans doute qu'il se sentait brave, et la
confiance qu'il avait dans son poing avait ramené le calme
dans son esprit. Tous les soirs il se met au lit intrépide-
ment, et l'âme sereine; et tous deux nous dormons en paix
jusqu'au jour."

ANALYTICAL TABLE.

---

[1] Observation. A mesure que nous avançons dans nos entretiens, la
matière devient plus riche, et les idées abondent. C'est pour cette raison
qu'à partir du chapitre XV, je ne donne plus une analyse détaillée des
chapitres: cette table serait interminable. J'indiquerai seulement les prin-
cipaux points touchés dans mes leçons.

— Faut-il lire les originaux ? — Mes anglais. — Italiens, Allemands, Espagnols. — Les Français : liste plus complète. — Prose française, poésie anglaise, et les Grecs. — Les grands américains. — Liste réduite à quatorze noms. — Adieu à mes élèves. Tristesse.

CAUSERIES AVEC MES ELEVES,

BY

LAMBERT SAUVEUR.

THE book entitled " Causeries avec mes Elèves," published in August last, has been highly successful : more than one thousand copies have been sold in five months, the greater part of them in Boston.

The book has been noticed in many of the leading journals; but no adverse criticism has been made, unless that the method proposed is difficult to practise.

There are, however, in Boston, at the present time, ten or twelve teachers who employ the system with great success; and the author has not met a single instructor who did not express a desire to adopt it, after it had been fully explained.

In future, especial attention will be given to the preparing of teachers. They will attend my daily class, and during the latter part of the school year will also be directly trained in methods of practical instruction.

To aid schools in making a trial of this system, I propose to give a single lesson to such as may wish to receive me. It will be the first lesson described in my pamphlet, "Introduction to the Teaching of Living Languages without Grammar or Dictionary." I will ask the principals of those schools to intrust to me, for an hour or two, fifteen or twenty of their pupils who do not understand French, and will then show in presence of the masters, and members of the committee, the practical working of the system.

This lesson will also be given in the same manner at Meionaon Hall, about the end of April, after my course of lectures is finished. Reporters for the newspapers will be specially invited, that they may be able to give the public their judgment.

The same lesson will be presented in New York and other cities, but chiefly in New England.

I would request the principals of schools who desire to receive me, to communicate with me at their earliest convenience, that I may dispose of my time to advantage.

I have been frequently asked to publish a book more simple than the "Causeries," intended especially for children. This is now in course of preparation, and will be issued in the month of May, under the title of "Causeries avec les Enfants."

I present some notices of the "Causeries avec mes Elèves," which have appeared in the public journals.

NOTICES OF THE PRESS.

From the Nation.

Dr. Sauveur has been well known for some years in New Haven and Boston as a highly successful teacher of French in the School of Modern Languages, of which he and Professor Heness are the conductors. The method pursued in the school with such excellent results differs from that usually followed, in that the pupil learns the language which he undertakes to acquire without the aid of grammar or dictionary, purely as a spoken language, and much in the same way that a child would learn it. English is banished from the class-room; the time is used in conversation, beginning with such simple elements as the familiar objects in the room may afford, and the vocabulary is formed by degrees, every day fixing in the memory the words already learned and adding others, until, in a surprisingly short time, the learner finds himself carrying on some animated discussion, of limited range to be sure at first, but with a sufficient command of his new language for the purpose. Pronunciation is acquired and the ear formed at the same time, without the confusion which the written form of French or German is apt to create at first.

The risk in following this system doubtless is, that in the hands of an incompetent teacher, or of one only moderately interested in his work, it may degenerate into Ollendorffism. It is no part of Dr. Sauveur's theory, however, that the learner should spend his time in ringing the changes upon "the handsome waistcoat of the bad carpenter" and the like. So far as the pupil's vocabulary goes, he contends that it should be made the vehicle of thoughts, that other mental faculties besides the memory should be stimulated, and that the easy use of language should be gained by exciting interest in the actual exchange of ideas, as well as by practising the mere mechanical glibness at which other *vivâ-voce* systems aim. How this important end is to be secured is shown by the little book which he has just published, made up of such conversations as he holds with his pupils in his every-day classes.

These "Causeries avec mes Elèves" open with a chapter, sufficiently simple, on "The Fingers," in which the teacher—qui
"montre sans cesse," as a note informs us—begins: "Voilà le
doigt. Regardez. Voilà l'index, voilà le doigt du milieu," and so
on. Naturally enough the pupil learns to count; one finger being
longer or stronger than another introduces the simpler comparisons of adjectives; distinctions of gender are noted; and, in
short, many of the elements of speech are placed at his command
by variations on the original theme. In succeeding chapters "The
Hands," "The Arms," "The Shoulders," "The Class-Room,"
"To-day, Yesterday, and To-morrow," are in the same way made
to serve each as the text for a discussion—one may fairly say
"a talk," so easy is its flow—in which new words and new con-
structions are given to the pupil, in a natural order and in rapid
succession. The book itself, however, is only a part, and not the
most important one, of the system:—

"It must be borne in mind that I always suppose the pupil to
be led by an attentive and intelligent teacher. No book can quite
take the place of oral instruction. Besides, my work is only a
portion of the lesson to be given; it can guide the teacher, suggest to him ten questions where I give one, and also inspire the
pupil, excite him to ask questions, and awaken his curiosity.
This is the whole system of Socrates. If the teacher spend eight
days on one of my lessons, he will have employed the time well.
They ask me also if the pupil is to read my book with his teacher.
. . . If you wish to have my advice on this point, do as follows
at the commencement: give your pupils the book to read at home,
as a preparation for your teaching, but forbid them to open it in
the class. Their ear alone must be occupied there. When they
are before you, put to them a hundred questions on the lesson of
the book; and, if you wish, read to them yourself a page from the
book, and make them understand every thing without ever pronouncing a word of English. There is the secret and the condition of success."

As before, "un maître qui montre sans cesse," who can invent
such questions on simple objects as shall fix the attention and
quicken the faculties, is indispensable. It is a part of Dr. Sauveur's system, however, that the master should do even more
than this, and that he should give a living interest to his lessons by
making literature, history, and criticism the subjects of his conversations, as soon as the pupil is advanced enough for such dis-

cussion. Thus, for many of his chapters he takes some fable from
La Fontaine as his theme, recites and comments upon it, illustrates
it by historical reference or digresses to some inviting collateral
topic, — all, be it understood, in question and answer, skilfully and
sometimes even artistically managed. Molière, Pascal, a humor-
ous passage or two from Töpffer, in the same way supply the texts
for chapters, which give variety and freshness to what is usually
a monotonous and dry road.

The result of all this is a book of an entirely different order
from the familiar book of exercises. It must be said, also, that
for its successful use it requires a teacher of a different class from
the ordinary teacher of French. The book gives the heads for a
series of spirited conversations; but they are to be conversations
between eager and curious pupils and a cultivated master, who is
able to give to their questions answers which shall instruct and
satisfy the mind as well as meet grammatical requirements. It
is only here and there that we find the teacher of French who,
like Dr. Sauveur, can make his exercise a *conférence* on the master-
pieces of poetry and the drama. For this reason we are less confident than Dr. Sauveur as to the immediate practicability of the
revolution which his enthusiasm foresees in the method of learning
modern languages, though not less persuaded of its desirableness.
As for the dead languages, the instruction in which he would also
reform in the same manner, his efforts will at any rate help, we
trust, to strengthen the movement for freeing the path of the student from the mass of grammatical pedantry which has long ob-
structed it, and for opening to him the literature of those tongues,
while he still has the time and spirit for its full enjoyment.

From the Boston Daily Advertiser.

Professor Lambert Sauveur, whose great success in teaching
French without the use of grammar or dictionary is so well known
here and in New Haven, has in press a volume of conversations, —
"Causeries avec mes Elèves," — which show the character and
extent of the subjects to which he directs the attention of his
pupils. They have nothing in common with the stiff, useless, silly
questions and answers given in Ollendorff and most phrase-books,
but are pleasant and intelligent conversations about literature,
sentiment, art, and nature; especially about French authors and
their peculiar characteristics. These " Causeries " are not intended

as a text-book to be literally followed or learned by heart, but as an assistant to both pupil and teacher, a guide to subjects and methods of conversation, as well as a pleasant book for reading by those who seek pure and graceful French.

The chapter on " Les Livres à Lire " is interesting, as showing the taste in literature of an accomplished French gentleman and teacher, and his judgment as to books especially desirable for young French students. He agrees fully with all that Mr. Emerson says in his essay on Books, but adds to those which Mr. Emerson recommends many French authors whom Mr. Emerson, being English in his taste, had not mentioned. The list contains Greek and Latin, and English and French classics, and is gathered from a wide extent of modern literature. Dr. Sauveur gives a prominent place to French histories and French memoirs ; but in English poetry, one is surprised to find that he recommends " Aurora Leigh," which cannot rank high either as a story, a poem, or a scheme of social reform. From French romances he makes careful selections for his pupils, and his criticisms and advice must be of real value to young readers, and, indeed, to any one who likes to have the sheep separated from the goats in literature, and so to be spared the possible dangers of a mixed flock.

Dr. Sauveur's system of teaching is his own : he is an enthusiast in regard to it ; and everybody who ever attended even one of his lectures is a convert to it. He uses no text-books ; he imposes no tasks : he requires only that his pupils shall be present, shall miss no lesson, drop no link in the chain that leads them so easily and pleasantly from ignorance to complete mastery of the French language. If the pupil is present, that is enough ; he, as teacher, will insure attention, interest, spirit, and steady improvement. And he certainly accomplishes all this. Some of his pupils have already become teachers, and to them his volume of " Causeries " will be of the greatest value ; for, although they are perfectly familiar with his system, yet his enthusiasm and his uncommon powers of conversation cannot be imparted ; and these, with his genius for his profession, must always make him pre-eminent as a teacher.

In addition to the volume of conversations, Dr. Sauveur is publishing a pamphlet on the subject of " Teaching without Grammar or Dictionary," which will interest not his pupils only, but all teachers and students of any language. As the works of the masters have preceded grammars, so should the study of the masters precede the study of grammar. After the language is well known, the study of grammar becomes a work of intelligence, full of serious enjoyment: before that time it is useless. This rejection of grammars is only for those who teach and learn the spoken language, and is not intended as a criticism on the method of teaching in the universities. In speaking of the poverty of the books commonly used in teaching French, Dr. Sauveur writes:—

" Why, then, are all these books so poor? The reason for it is still in the great defect, the teaching by grammars and dictionaries. One looks only for words and thinks only of teaching words. One has no ideas, and attaches no price to ideas, and yet ideas alone can lead to the knowledge even of words. I will be more explicit in relating a fact of my experience. While at New Haven I taught a select class formed of the tutors of Yale, during four months and a half. They spent two hours with me five times a week. After this time they were almost as French as I, and I have afterwards passed with them more than one evening without hearing a word of English pronounced. The conversation was so animated and so interesting that I believed myself in the midst of a select club of France. I never taught words to these gentlemen; I only took care to communicate to them my ideas and to receive theirs: after a month's time their ear was accustomed to the sounds of the language, and we discussed a tragedy of Sophocles, or of Æschylus, or of Euripides, of Racine, or of Shakespeare; we talked about France, England, America; reasoned upon an oration of Cicero, upon Bacon or La Rochefoucauld, upon men and things; one of my pupils, who was studying philosophy deeply, spoke to us of John Stuart Mill, and of the contemporaneous philosophers of England; we conversed about Renan and Littré; another of my pupils, who had been an officer in the civil war, related to us his experience; a third made me acquainted with the different churches of this country, &c. This is not a hundredth part of our conversations. I would forget that I was teaching, and they would forget that they were studying French: they have told me so twenty times. And yet they were studying it admirably, since they said nothing in English, and since, after four months and a half, the acquisition of the language was made for ever. Is it not clear, then, that the means of learning the words of a language is not to think about them, but to produce ideas constantly, using for instrument only words of the language one is studying? I defy any thoughtful man to gainsay me."

MR. EDITOR, — I have just finished reading a pamphlet called
"Teaching without Grammar or Dictionary," written by Professor L. Sauveur, and coming from the press of Mr. John Wilson of
Cambridge. This pamphlet, well printed and neat in appearance,
is designed to explain Professor Sauveur's system of teaching, and
is to accompany a book entitled "Causeries avec mes Élèves," to
appear in a week or ten days, and which is a work to serve as a
guide for those studying French. The pamphlet consists of
seventy-five pages, divided into six chapters, with the headings as
follows: The first lesson; The system; How the book is to be
used; The grammar; Conversation; Four chapters from " Causeries avec mes Élèves." These chapters are followed by the analytical table of the book, presenting in detail a vast range of subjects.
In the chapter on grammar, Professor Sauveur writes, addressing
those teachers who have practised his method for some time, and
speaking of grammars written in English : —

"I assure you that you will not open one of them. Your pupils
will be already acquainted with the grammar by practice, and will
be ready to form with you the rules of the language. If you wish,
open in their presence a French grammar of France, which does
not know of the existence of English, the smallest you can find,
and give yourself the pleasure of proving together that you all
know the grammar. They would laugh heartily, these pupils who
speak and write French without having heard even the words
French grammar; who have talked with you during a year on
every subject, and exchanged with you in French thousands and
thousands of ideas; who are acquainted with the books of Corneille, Molière, Racine, Pascal, La Rochefoucauld, Victor Hugo,
George Sand, Guizot, Thiers, and twenty others, — they would
laugh heartily, I say, if you wish to teach them that there are
three accents in French, that there are only two genders ; that a
cedilla is put under the *c* in certain cases; that our language has
no declensions like the Latin ; that *dans, de, avec,* &c., are French
prepositions ; that one must say *l'Amérique,* and not *le Boston,* but
simply *Boston* without the article; that *mon, notre, votre,* are possessive adjectives ; that *qui? que? quoi?* are interrogative pronouns ;
if you wished to teach them that the verb *aller* is irregular ; that
we say in the present, *je vais,* in the future, *j'irai,* &c. ; that the
verb *pouloir* takes no preposition ; that we say *je ne veux pas étudier,*

and not *je ne veux pas d'étudier* or *à étudier une* ' French Grammar.'
But there is the grammar. Do you not see that they know it all,
and that it only remains for you to examine what the most intelligent men examine everywhere, the great, the difficult and curious
questions of the languages ? "

As one of the pupils of Professor Sauveur, I would say that surely
we never knew when we learned all this : we must have breathed
it in with the atmosphere ; and the very idea of any of us being
satisfied to go back now to the study of the language by grammar
rules and dictionary would indeed cause a laugh. There was always a fascination about our lessons, holding the whole class spell-
bound, as it were. I have often thought since, and almost with
remorse, of our many times keeping our teacher after the expira-
tion of the hour, so interested were we in what we were doing.
We did not know the word fatigue, and did not consider that he,
after his long exertion, might perhaps know its meaning only too
well ; and I fear he may have sometimes had occasion to wish his
class were not quite so enthusiastic. Indeed, many a time nothing
but ocular proof would convince us that it was time to leave the
class-room. No one of his pupils can help fully sympathizing
with the following words, recently pronounced in one of our leading papers.*

There cannot be a better substitute for those unable to attend his
classes than this book ; in reading the few chapters from it that
have been given as examples in the pamphlet, our class lessons
have been repeatedly brought before my mind ; they are not here
in their full completeness, — how were that possible ? but he has
touched upon so many points, and in such a way, too, as to open
to the reader or teacher who uses the book an endless field of
thought and inquiry. To thank him for placing such a help and
assistance within the reach of so many, is the desire of one who
has experienced great pleasure no less than benefit as a pupil.

From the Boston Globe.

Had we known nothing of the truly wonderful work done by
Professor Lambert Sauveur in the teaching of the French language, the title of his book alone would have been sufficient to
create an earnest desire to become acquainted with its contents.

* See notice from " Advertiser," page 6, " Dr. Sauveur's system of teaching," &c., &c.

"Causeries avec mes Elèves," "Talks with my Pupils," not recitations from them. The curiosity excited by the title at once gives place to an ever-deepening interest as we open and read. Immediately we are in a French atmosphere: the professor himself appears before us, as in our first lesson, when speaking with all the eloquence of voice, eye, and gesture, he led us onward by easy and rapid steps, until all at once we found ourselves talking in a tongue before unknown to us. Thus is the French language taught without grammar or dictionary. This system of Professor Sauveur is certainly a decided step forward in the art of teaching. It merits the serious attention of every earnest, thoughtful teacher. Can his book and method be introduced with advantage into our schools? Those who are teaching according to the old system will hardly believe that this can be done, but let such carefully examine "Causeries avec mes Elèves" and the pamphlet which accompanies it, and we think that they will acknowledge the system to be in itself admirable, whatever objections they may see to the adoption of it in their own work. And what are these objections? The time given in our schools to the study of a language is necessarily quite limited: perhaps only two or three hours each week can be devoted to French. In many cases also text-books already in use cannot easily be thrown aside. We think these difficulties apparent rather than real. Professor Sauveur's book, in the hands of an intelligent teacher, would prove a great saving of time and labor; with it, the two or three hours each week would produce results far more satisfactory than the same time spent with the ordinary text-books. But suppose the grammar must be retained, a small part of each recitation hour could be given to "Causeries avec mes Elèves," and thus used, although such is not its true place, it would soon become an invaluable aid to teachers in awakening interest among their pupils, for its purely French influence is irresistible. Once let it find its way into the class-room, and we predict that it will not readily be given up. Let teachers try it, using it, as has been suggested by Professor Sauveur in his pamphlet, from which we quote below:—

"It must be borne in mind that I always suppose the pupil to be led by an attentive and intelligent teacher. No book can quite take the place of oral instruction. Besides, my work is only a portion of the lesson to be given: it can guide the teacher, suggest to him ten questions where I give one, and also inspire the pupil, excite him to ask questions, and awaken his curiosity. This is the whole system of Socrates. If the teacher spend eight days upon one of my lessons, he will have employed the time well. I am asked if the pupil is to read my book with his teacher. My dear brother teachers, I have neither the right nor the pretension to prescribe to you any thing. Put your experience by the side of mine, and do whatever you deem most useful to your pupil. If, however, you wish to have my advice on this point, do as follows at the commencement: Give your pupils the book to read at home, as a preparation for your teaching, but forbid them to open it in the class; their ear alone must be occupied there. When they are before you, put to them a hundred questions on the lesson of the book, and, if you wish, read to them yourself a page from the book, and make them understand every thing without ever pronouncing a word of English. There is the secret and the condition of success."

From the Boston Traveller.

CAUSERIES AVEC MES ELÈVES. — We have received the work of Lambert Sauveur, Ph. D., LL.D., bearing the above title, and the accompanying pamphlet, " Introduction to the Teaching of Living Languages without Grammar or Dictionary," and are at a loss to find fitting terms to speak the deserved commendations for the books. Professor Sauveur has opened a new field of instruction in America, and he will soon find hundreds as enthusiastic as himself concerning his method of teaching. Reading the " Causeries," we were simply fascinated and carried on, page after page, with irresistible attraction, and, reaching the later chapters, found ourselves paying the highest tribute in our power to the lecturer's ability, in the interest which had been excited in the contents. The attraction which would come from the matter in the volume when presented by word of mouth by the teacher, we can well imagine would be manifold more than that gained by reading. We heartily commend the books, and are glad to give the following communication sent us concerning them : —

" DEAR MR. EDITOR, — I wish to call the attention of your readers to a book bearing the title, ' Causeries avec mes Elèves,' recently from the press. It is designed for the assistance of those teaching French by the system of the author, Professor Lambert Sauveur.

This system is the conversational method, in which he has met with such unparalleled success. To describe the book allow me to quote from an editorial which appeared not long since in the ' Boston Advertiser : '

"' These conversations have nothing in common,' " &c.

This book is one which would be of great help to those teaching French. Let it be used as Professor Sauveur directs, or where this cannot be done, owing to teachers being constrained to employ the grammar and other text-books, as in public schools, &c., it may be used in connection with the grammar to very great advantage. Speaking with a young lady attending one of our high schools, and belonging to a class where this book has already been used at the same time with the grammar, she said that the portion of the hour devoted to the " Causeries " was by far the most interesting ; that at that point of the lesson the ears and the minds of the whole class were opened, and that here the teacher always found a ready attention. Our teachers are too often given a book, confined and restricted to that alone, and yet we expect to find their pupils prepared to turn their knowledge to practical account in after life. How can there be much real practicability in such instruction ? It has been aptly, I think, likened to shutting a bird into a cage, surrounding him with young birds, and then wondering why these little ones are not taught to fly.

If pupils were not required to learn so much that is useless, — as, for instance, formal, dry rules of grammar, — the same time might be devoted to something to be of real value and good to them afterwards. These " Causeries " are to be used as a nucleus, a starting-point, to be enlarged upon and opened up by the teacher. They are to serve as a guide, and as such must be found invaluable to both teacher and pupil.

From the Hartford Times.

As the title indicates, this is a book of conversations with the pupils of Dr. Sauveur, a gentleman who has already attained an enviable reputation in this country as a teacher of the French language. In order to appreciate the importance of this publication, it is desirable to know something of the system of instruction for which he has so signal a genius, and which has met with so great popularity.

Most fortunate those who will receive the book as a pleasant review and *souvenir* of class hours, while still highly favored are those beyond the reach of his voice, who may enroll themselves his pupils by a perusal of its pages.

It is no exaggeration to report, that, after a few months' study, those under his charge are enabled to speak, read, and write in French with ease and correctness. Beginning with no knowledge of the language, they speak from the first lesson upon the most familiar topics, rapidly increasing their vocabulary at every meeting till they are capable of discussing history, literature, and philosophy. This result is also attained without the use of grammar or dictionary, Dr. Sauveur guiding his pupils in a new and delightful pathway, where are no long lists of vocabularies to bewilder, or tiresome rules and conjugations for them to stumble over. This fact of itself is sufficient to commend the system to all young students to whom the grammar is a *bête noir* of the most hostile type; while even those who hold to the old text-books, and are afraid to desert the beaten highway, must be convinced of its superiority, when their attention is directed to the rapidity and thoroughness with which the language is mastered. Not that the grammar is discarded altogether, but the study of it is postponed to a later stage of progress, when the pupil can better understand and appreciate its significance.

In an introductory pamphlet, Dr. Sauveur has given his ideas upon this subject in the " Teaching of Living Languages." Here he takes the same ground as many eminent scholars of the day, and which is destined before long to be universally accepted in our schools and colleges. A perfect enthusiast in his profession, with characteristic modesty he ascribes his remarkable success in teaching to his method or system, for which he does not claim originality, but is happy to class himself a disciple of Socrates and Montaigne. Instead of a tedious recital of rules and exceptions, a confused idea of *y's, en's,* and *ne's,* a memorizing of such aspiring sentences as " Have you the hat ? " " I have the hat," the pupil is led to converse in a familiar way on the most interesting and instructive subjects.

These conversations are as far as possible now transferred to print in the volume just published, — " Causeries avec mes Élèves." While they lack the charm and enthusiasm which his personal presence imparts, they form a most delightful book for all lovers of pure and graceful French. It is an embodiment of forty-nine lessons, varied in the most charming manner by anecdotes, fables, criticisms of authors and distinguished people, choice extracts of poetry, history, and philosophy. Some chapters are replete with melody, as those on "The Bullfinch," "The Nightingale," and "The Swallow," and present most pleasing pictures of French country life. In the closing chapter Dr. Sauveur constitutes himself a "professor of books," of which, says Emerson, "no chair is so much wanted," and gives a most valuable selection for those unacquainted with French literature.

In short, all who desire the conversation and society of a most cultivated and distinguished scholar, may find them in these "Causeries," by which the author has now introduced himself. They meet a demand which has long been felt for such a book, and ought to supersede the old text-books, as a manual for all teachers of the language. The reader will there find an answer to all questions which will naturally be suggested on the topics presented, and cannot fail to enjoy the perusal of its pages. Entirely original and attractive, a wide circulation is deserved and predicted for it.

From the Salem Gazette.

The mere announcement of this book by Dr. L. Sauveur is sufficient to call to its attention his host of friends, admirers, and pupils; while his high reputation in New Haven and Boston will ensure for it a wide circulation among all interested in the French language. Any one who has had the pleasure of being present at one of his class lessons, to see the enthusiasm of both instructor and pupils, will understand his peculiar genius for teaching, and hail this book with delight as the key to the remarkable success to which he has attained. It will open a new field in the study of the language, and flowers will spring up where before was arid sand. Dr. Sauveur belongs to the school of Object Teachers, now so popular in all departments of instruction. While Miss Peabody is endeavoring by Froebel's method to change the old ways of beginning the education of children, while Sunday schools all over the land are seeking with maps and pictures to make the study of the Bible simple and attractive, and every department of science is being made fascinating, on this same advanced platform Dr. Sauveur appears, to demonstrate that the French language can be taught without grammar or dictionary. It was

Heine who said that if the Romans had been obliged to learn the Latin grammar they would never have had time to conquer the world; and the French grammar with its *y's* and *en's*, its *si's* and its *ne's* is the *bête noir* of all who attempt to conquer this language. In a pamphlet introductory to "Causeries avecmes Elèves," Dr. Sauveur, with Montaigne for his authority, takes the same ground in regard to the teaching of French as Mr. George B. Emerson, in an address before the Boston Social Science Association in 1867, has taken in reference to the English and Latin grammar.

An instance which Dr. Sauveur relates of a class of tutors in Yale, who, after four and a half months' study, were enabled to converse with him in French on all literary and philosophical subjects, is only one of many showing the astonishing progress made by his pupils. This experience is in striking contrast to that of most French students, — well illustrated by that of the "American Girl Abroad," who, after a long study of the language at boarding-school, on arriving in Paris, could only bring to her command the words, "Have you the hammer of the carpenter, or the anvil of the blacksmith ?"

It is not himself but his system which the author of this book wishes to introduce; nature's system in fact, the same in which all children learn to speak and understand their mother-tongue. Not by dry rules and definitions, but by an acquaintance with the names and uses of the most familiar objects, does the student without any study of text-books advance by an ascending scale to a point where the grammar is readily understood and mastered. His book is an embodiment of his lessons from first to last, and to those acquainted with his system will be most valuable as a guide in teaching; while the wide range of subjects which it embraces makes it a most attractive and readable volume. The French is pure and beautiful, and such chapters as those on "The Bullfinch," "The Swallow," and "The Nightingale" are remarkable for grace and poetry. Many readers of French are in doubt about what books to read, and in one of the chapters or lessons Dr. Sauveur has made a selection which, from a man of his wide culture, will be invaluable to young students. Could the author of this book or a teacher of his system occupy a position in regard to the French language which Mr. Walter Smith occupies in the teaching of drawing, with "Causeries avec mes Elèves" for a guide, it would be safe to predict a revolution in teaching French in our schools which would yield the most astonishing and satisfactory results. Could the rising generation appreciate the immense advantage of this new system, they would with one accord rebel against committing to memory long lists of definitions, dry rules, and conjugations of verbs. Will not those having its education in charge become acquainted with Dr. Sauveur's book and system in comparison with the senseless and tedious text-books now in use in our schools?

From the Portland Transcript.

This book deserves more than an ordinary notice in its introduction to the public, not only on account of its merit and originality, but because it is an illustration of a new method of teaching French without grammar or dictionary. Its author Professor Sauveur, a gentleman of the highest education and culture, has had brilliant success in teaching, according to this improved system, in Boston and elsewhere, and writes this book as a *souvenir* of conversations held between him and his pupils, hoping at the same time that other teachers may profit by his experience, and effect a radical change in the manner of teaching. In conducting his classes, Professor Sauveur supposes that French is the only medium of communication between him and his scholars, and from the first hour French alone is spoken. As the book shows, the conversation begins with simple and familiar objects, going on in a regular chain, adding new words to the scholar's vocabulary at each lesson, till at the end of the term he is able to converse upon literary, philosophical, and social subjects with ease and fluency. The method is simply the natural way of learning, as a child learns its mother-tongue by becoming familiar with the names of objects around it, acquiring new words each day as new ideas come, and opening a book only after the ear has become accustomed to the sounds of the language. The practicability of the system is well established by Dr. Sauveur; and, when one has seen the interest and enthusiasm awakened in his classes, the wonder is that we could have gone on so long in the old stupid routine of studying French with grammars, learning dry rules, stiff questions and answers that no occasion ever seems to make available, and giving the pupil in the end only a smattering of the language. The explanation here given is necessary in order to show the character and value of "Causeries avec mes Elèves." The student and teacher will find the book useful and attractive, showing by its natural conversations how the language is acquired step by step, and will gain here not only a knowledge of speaking pure and correct French, but a wealth of ideas and improvement of mind. The reader of cultivated taste will enjoy the book from the interesting topics of which it treats, its fine criticisms upon books and authors, its animated style, and the elegance of its French. Every chapter has its own merit, but some are worthy of a more than general notice. Those upon "La Fontaine" and his fables are full of beauty and instruction; the chapters upon the Bullfinch, Swallow, and Nightingale, exceedingly graceful and poetical, giving a true picture of French country life; the pages upon "La Patrie," "Pascal," and "Socrates," elevated and sublime; while the opinions upon our own English books and authors show the literary taste and discrimination of the writer. The pamphlet entitled "Introduction to the Teaching of Languages without Grammar or Dictionary" explains Professor Sauveur's system in a clear and able manner and is designed to accompany "Causeries avec mes Elèves," showing its value as text-book to teachers and scholars.

From the Index (Boston).

A NEW METHOD OF TEACHING FRENCH.

I shall name it the *talking* system. I shall call it French *yeast* of a very superior quality, that never fails to set the atoms of the dullest brain and the slowest tongue in motion, when once introduced.

Professor Sauveur, who is the author of this remarkable school, starts with the supposition that persons unlearned in the French language are as truly children in that department of knowledge as the infant is ignorant of its mother's vocabulary. One is as helpless as the other, as dependent as the other; and both must be led into the great mystery of speech by like methods. The mother talks to the little one by means of the love in her eyes, by the smile on her lips, by kisses and caresses, and by every conceivable gesture, till it begins to comprehend her spoken words and lisp them after her. She brings no other means to aid her in this task of speech-making. In a similar way, with no other methods than the mother takes with her into the nursery, — armed with no grammars, or dictionaries, or other outward means of proceeding, — Professor Sauveur appears before a class of educated English men and women to give them their first lesson in

French. They are not familiar with a word of his language, and he is nearly as ignorant of theirs. Each is boxed up in a separate world.

Before I attempt to show the process by which these two tongues are to mingle and run together, and their speakers to become familiar as people of a common country, I must mention the very significant fact that, in this school, *every thing* depends upon the teacher. " As is the teacher, so is the school," is an old saying, and answers very well for school-keeping ; but it is not emphasized enough by half for this method, which must be conducted by a specially gifted instructor, or there can be no school at all, either good or bad. Professor Sauveur is an accomplished conversationist; but that is not all. He is a man of letters, possessing wit, genius, culture, and vast information, which beam all over his face, and speak in every motion. This exterior man is so promising he awakens the curiosity of the class at once, and inspires them with intense eagerness to gain access to the rich jewels contained in his intellectual storehouse. They forget the rough and rugged labor that intervenes, and grasp with eagerness any tools he may put into their hands, with which to make their way.

This class may be composed of children, but it is more likely to be of matured men and women ; graduates from Harvard, students from Yale, and persons who have spent years searching for the hidden treasures of the heart and intellect. Teacher and pupils are both familiar with the truths and beauties of Plato and Socrates, only their ideas are draped in different costumes, — one wears French clothes, the other English. They come together for the first time. The teacher prefers, perhaps, to speak about Tyndall's last address, which contains the "promise and potency of terrestrial life." The class, quite likely, are thinking in the same direction. They, too, would choose to discourse upon this theme. It would not be surprising if the teacher should articulate some thought from Tyndall. Neither would it be astonishing if the class before him surmised what he said, though they comprehended not a spoken word. But they read the soul that moves over the face, beams in the eye, lights the brow, and lifts the hand. Already a means of communication has been opened by signs and gestures. These are to prepare the way for words : they are to do the talking before words are learned, and are to be an accompaniment for words through all future conversation. Were Mr. Tyndall present, the teacher would point to him, and say, "un homme sage." This would be in keeping with the philosophy of his system, which is to express the supreme thoughts in the mind at the moment. But Tyndall is absent; so the teacher holds up one finger, and says, "Un doigt:" two French words are learned. He holds up two fingers, and says, "Deux doigts," — three French words are learned. The parts of the finger are examined; the different fingers, — "l'index," "le pouce." They are counted, and a great deal of conversation is carried on concerning them, which lasts an hour.

The second and third lessons continue with the hand, the arm, shoulder, the hair, and objects that are visible about the room. In all this time not a word of English has been spoken; but a great variety of gestures has been employed, and every word learned has been a powerful magnet, gathering to itself innumerable companions.

For a few lessons, these persons with ideas are treated much like children with none. They are so helpless that only such subjects can be treated as can be illustrated. But in the fourth lesson we observe in the professor's new grammar, "Causeries avec mes Elèves," such sentences as the following: "Connaissez-vous Socrate?" "Est-il vivant ou mort?" "Dans l'Iliade d'Homère vous voyez l'impitoyable Achille lui-même respecter les cheveux blancs du vieux Priam" (the lesson has been "les cheveux"). From this time onward there is a wide divergence from the course that would have been pursued with children. The teacher begins to unlock the intellect, appeal to the thought and sympathy of his pupils. A few common words have put them more nearly on a level, and they now have the key with which to enter each the soul of the other. The interest deepens. The pupils are not only accumulating column upon column of words, but they are discoursing henceforth upon real, living subjects.

They sit about their teacher as one could imagine the pupils of Plato to have done, in the quiet groves of the Academy. Are they learning French, studying the Fables of La Fontaine, the writings öf Montaigne, or the radicalism of Wendell Phillips? It would be difficult to tell. One moment they are talking of the future tense, or the use of the subjunctive: the next we hear: "Quel livre de M. Emerson préférez-vous?" or "Quelle est la pièce de Shakspeare que vous avez le plus lue?" or, "Pouvons-nous mesurer la grandeur morale de Socrate, mesdames?"

Who would not struggle bravely to gain the means whereby to converse upon such lofty themes with a profound scholar, a graceful and sympathetic conversationist? Who would not take French lessons, if for no other purpose than to study the literature of the world, to be filled with new thoughts and inspiration, and to be fitting one's self as a genial companion.

There has not been a word of English heard in all these lessons, neither have there been any French translations made in English.

The class read from French books; and, when a sentence or paragraph is met that is not understood, the teacher makes the explanation in French, in the same way that he treats any subject of conversation. Thus they learn to think and feel in French, — the whole mind becomes saturated with French, and the ideas are clothed in French terms. So great is the gift of this remarkable teacher, and so superior his system of instruction, that before he parts with his pupils he has given them, not only the technical words of his language, but taken them into the heart of the French literature, into the character of his countrymen, and into the soul of French life. They find they have duplicated themselves, or added a French nature to their American. They are two times one; and they scarcely know which *one* they are the more.

The inquiry naturally arises, Can this new method be made to benefit the masses as well as individuals? Can there be more than one Sauveur, and can his system be introduced into general education, English as well as French? That there is need of this, no one will deny who visits our school-rooms, and listens to the dull and monotonous "lesson-saying" that is dragging its weary self along day after day, as regularly as the weaver's shuttle, and just about as intelligently, — who realizes the fact that not one teacher in fifty is able to command the attention of a class for any length of time by means of any real conversation, — who goes into society and witnesses the miserable botch-work that is made when people attempt to hold what they *call* a conversation.

We are introducing many new arts into our education. If there be room for one more, "the talking art," its success would be sure under the guiding hand of such a master as Professor Sauveur. Ought not the "talking art" to precede all others?

1-8   The [...] the first lesson
27   ask only earnest questions
28   connect scrupulously the
        question in such manner that
        one gives rise to ans?..